The Impact of Christianity

on the Socioeconomic Development of Nations

Romel Hilaire

To all wounded nations that still long for justice.

To the men and women who pray in silence for their country's well-being.

To the leaders who believe in governing with integrity.

To every church that chooses not only to shine but also to become a source of illumination.

And especially to the next generation, because their faith will have the power to build a better world.

About the Book

This book examines the influence that Christian principles have had, and may continue to have, on the socioeconomic development of nations. Through a historical, ethical, and cultural analysis, it explores how Christian values, honesty, responsibility, diligent work, social justice, and solidarity have been fundamental to building prosperous and sustainable societies. The author argues that, far from being merely a private belief, Christianity can act as a transformative force when its principles are applied to areas such as education, politics, economy, and institutions. The book also presents concrete examples of countries that, by integrating or adopting these values, have shown notable advances in social well-being, Political stabilization, and economic growth.

INTRODUCTION

WE FIND OURSELVES in a time of great uncertainty. Despite the world's unprecedented connectivity,

We are divided by crises related to identity, inequality, violence, and distrust of institutions. Solutions seem to elude both leaders and ordinary citizens. Given this complex landscape, one question arises: what contribution could Christianity make to create societies that are more humane, just, and sustainable?

This book does not arise from abstract theory but from a practical conviction: that Christian faith, when integrated into culture, the economy, politics, and education, has the power to profoundly transform a nation's destiny.

My goal is not to promote religious proselytism or advocate for a modern theocracy. On the contrary, my aim is to show how the universal values of Christianity, such as compassion, integrity, justice, service, and humility, have been and can continue to be foundational pillars for social and economic development.

Throughout these pages, you will explore ideas, real stories, biblical principles, and concrete examples in which faith did not remain confined to temples; it became action, institution, and living culture. You will see that nations that have embraced these values have prospered not only economically but also in terms of dignity, cohesion, and resilience.

This work also invites us to reconsider the role of faith in the public sphere, not as an imposition but as a source of inspiration. It further leads us to understand that a country's success is measured not only by its productive capacity but by the principles on which it stands.

TABLE OF CONTENTS

CHAPTER ONE

Christian Ethics and Work

IT RAISES A CRUCIAL QUESTION: What can sustain a nation's progress beyond its natural resources or political power? This book offers a bold answer: when applied collectively, Christian principles provide an ethical and practical foundation capable of guiding nations toward development that is sustainable, just, and rooted in solidarity.

Far from being only a personal religion or a system of spirituality centered on the individual, Christianity has, throughout history, demonstrated its capacity to influence society positively. The teachings of Jesus offer a profound perspective on topics such as the intrinsic worth of the human person, social justice, the importance of honest work, and the principles of forgiveness and compassion as essential foundations for harmonious coexistence. The Bible addresses not only matters of faith but also economic issues, political and administrative leadership, and social equity. As expressed in Psalm 33:12:

"Blessed is the nation whose God is the Lord."

Lessons from the Past

In Europe, countries with a Protestant tradition, such as Switzerland, Norway, and the Netherlands, experienced an economic transformation that coincided with the sixteenth-century Reformation. Max Weber, in his classic work "The Protestant Ethic and the Spirit of Capitalism," argues that the Protestant emphasis on individual responsibility, diligent work, and prudent stewardship was fundamental to the development of modern capitalism. Although this view has its critics, it is undeniable that the Christian worldview significantly shaped financial, educational, and legal institutions in the West.

In South Korea

The example of South Korea is one of the clearest cases showing how the values, principles, and structures fostered by Christianity had a significant impact on its economic, social, and educational development. In less than seventy years, South Korea went from being among the poorest nations, ravaged by war, to becoming a leading global economic and technological power. Although various factors contributed to this progress, including government policies, industrialization, and foreign investment, the role of Christianity was key in three main areas: education, work ethic, and social progress.

Examples in Latin America and the Caribbean

In Latin America, a region historically affected by inequality and corruption, the growth of Christian communities has had a notable social impact. In countries such as Guatemala and Brazil, evangelical congregations have encouraged people to abandon addictions, promoted family reconciliation, and spurred ethical political participation. A study by Baylor University in Texas found that in Brazilian areas where evangelical churches are active in vulnerable zones, there is a tendency for levels of violence and poverty to decline, particularly among young people.

In the Dominican Republic, various Christian non-governmental organizations such as World Vision and Compassion International have achieved a positive impact in rural areas by fostering community development based on Christian values. Their work focuses on providing education, job training, food, and spiritual support.

In addition, during disaster situations, as in Port-au-Prince, Haiti, after the 2010 earthquake, local and international Christian churches became the first centers of humanitarian assistance. These organizations established support networks and coordinated shelters and food distribution. Christianity provided not only spiritual comfort but also an organized, practical, and effective response.

Applicable Biblical Foundations

Work and duty:

"If anyone is not willing to work, then neither shall he eat." This encourages a proactive ethic and avoids passive dependence.

Justice and governance:

"The people rejoice when the righteous are in power, but suffer when the wicked rule."

Economic integrity:

"The Lord detests dishonest scales, but delights in accurate weights."

This principle opposes corruption and promotes transparency in business and government.

Care for those in need:

"Whoever ignores the cry of the needy will also cry out and not be answered."

These passages indicate that a nation guided by Christian principles fosters a culture of responsibility, integrity, and service.

The Country's True Success

A nation's success is measured not only by its Gross Domestic Product (GDP) but also by the moral health of its people, the strength of its families, the balance of its laws, and the common purpose that unites them. Christianity, when lived as an authentic way of life and not used for political ends, can restore human dignity, revitalize the economy, and reconcile social divisions.

This book does not advocate imposing a religion or establishing a theocracy. It offers a strategic perspective grounded in universal biblical principles whose effectiveness has been proven throughout history. Just as a house needs foundations to remain firm, nations also need a solid anchor. Christianity can serve as that foundational pillar.

Christian Ethics and Work:

A Foundation for Progress and Dignity

From a Christian perspective, work is not seen as a punishment or only as an economic tool. Rather, it is understood as an expression of human purpose and dignity. From the very first pages of the Bible, God is portrayed as a worker: creator, designer, and organizer. Genesis 2:15 says:

Then the Lord God took the man and placed him in the Garden of Eden to cultivate it and care for it.

From the beginning, human beings were called to work and to care, not as slaves to a system but as collaborators with God in the development of the world.

The Christian Perspective on Work

The Christian work ethic is grounded in several key principles:

Diligence and excellence

"Put your heart into everything you do, as if it were for the Lord and not for people." (Colossians 3:23)

"Work should not be done out of obligation or in a mediocre way, but as an honorable act, with excellence and responsibility."

Honesty and Fairness

"Do not exploit the poor and needy worker." (Deuteronomy 24:14)

This underscores the importance of treating workers with justice and humanity, which is essential to eliminating labor exploitation and promoting ethical economic systems.

Productivity and Smart Management

"In the Parable of the Talents (Matthew 25:14-30), Jesus teaches that each person should grow what they have been given. This has direct implications for the economy, entrepreneurship, and responsible investment."

Unity and Community Spirit

Here is a paraphrase of the quote: "Whoever used to steal should stop, and instead work honestly with their hands so they can share with those in need."

Work not only dignifies the person, but it also helps build the social fabric, care for those in need, and uphold the common good.

History and Transformation: From Protestantism to Modernity

Max Weber showed that the work ethic promoted by Christianity, particularly its Protestant variant, fostered a culture of saving, responsibility, and productivity that helped shape the modern Western economy. Although aspects of his ideas are debated, many economists recognize that both industriousness and integrity have a direct impact on a country's economic success.

South Korea

Christianity arrived in South Korea in the eighteenth century but gained significant momentum in the nineteenth century with the arrival of Protestant missionaries. They not only spread the teachings of the gospel but also established modern schools, hospitals, universities, and literacy programs.

Christian teaching promoted individual dignity, equality between men and women, and the importance of personal responsibility. These principles contrasted with traditional Confucian hierarchies and laid the groundwork for a cultural shift that later helped South Korea adapt to modernization.

The missionaries also founded institutions that advanced science, innovation, and accessible education for all. These foundational principles were later used to spur economic growth.

Education and Human Capital: The Key to Development

One of Christianity's main contributions to South Korea's development was its focus on education. Christian missionaries established renowned universities, such as:

- Yonsei University (established in 1885)
- Ewha Womans University, established in 1886 as the country's first women's university

These institutions educated generations of leaders, scientists, entrepreneurs, and politicians who played an essential role in building the modern nation. Christianity taught that reading the Bible was fundamental, which encouraged mass literacy and made education a national priority.

After the Korean War (1950 to 1953), the country was left severely devastated. However, through an alliance between the Christian movement and the government, an education model centered on developing human capital was promoted. This strategy enabled South Korea to build high-value-added industries such as technology, electronics, and innovative scientific fields, despite having few natural resources.

Work Ethic and Economic Development

Christianity in South Korea also played an important role in establishing a firm work ethic grounded in biblical principles such as honesty, diligence, and stewardship.

Christian churches taught that work should be considered a service to both God and the community, promoting values such as:

- Individual responsibility
- Self-discipline and perseverance
- Saving and investment
- Community collaboration

These principles aligned with government policies in the 1960s and 1970s, when the country implemented a model of rapid industrialization. Christian communities played a crucial role by creating support networks among entrepreneurs, workers, and educators, which helped drive the growth of companies like Samsung, Hyundai, and LG, now recognized as global leaders.

Social Change and Governmental Stability

Another crucial aspect of the Christian contribution was its impact on strengthening democratic institutions and advancing social reforms. Churches played a significant role in:

- Protecting human rights
- Combating corruption
- Promoting social equity and equality

During the military dictatorship, Christian leaders played a key role by leading movements for freedom and civil rights. Their actions helped lay the groundwork for a more robust democracy. This institutional strength attracted foreign direct investment and strengthened the country's economic environment.

Notable Results

- The combined influence of Christian education, work ethic, and social reforms contributed significantly to South Korea's profound transformation.
- In 1960, South Korea's GDP per capita was just USD 79, comparable to some of the poorest countries in the world.
- Today, it exceeds USD 34,000 per person, and the country is a member of the OECD and the G20.
- The country stands out as one of the world's largest exporters of technology, automobiles, biotechnology, and culture.
- By fostering education, equity, work ethic, and innovation, Christianity had a notable impact on

building the social and human capital that made this extraordinary economic growth possible.

Conclusion

The example of South Korea shows how Christianity can function as a transformative engine for the socioeconomic development of nations. It not only offered a moral and spiritual foundation but also had a direct impact on education, productivity, innovation, and social cohesion. Thanks to these foundations, South Korea moved from extreme poverty to becoming a global power in less than three generations.

Christianity and Socioeconomic Development in Africa

Africa's history reflects a deep link between the arrival of Christianity and the beginning of transformative processes in education, society, and the economy. Although European colonization had negative impacts, it is undeniable that Christian missions were fundamental in developing school systems, hospitals, universities, printing presses, and community networks. These institutions gradually laid the groundwork for economic growth in several African countries.

Christianity in Africa not only focused on evangelization, but it also had a significant impact on mass literacy, human capital development, and the establishment of democratic institutions, all of which are essential for sustainable progress.

Education: The Most Impactful Legacy

During the nineteenth and twentieth centuries, Christian missionaries established schools, institutes, and universities across Africa. Their main goal was to teach reading and writing to facilitate Bible study. This sparked a wave of literacy that later became one of the key drivers of the continent's modernization.

Notable Examples:

Ghana

The first modern education systems were introduced by Presbyterian and Catholic missionaries.

The University of Ghana, originally founded by missionary institutions, has trained political, business, and scientific leaders.

Thanks to this educational focus, Ghana became one of the first West African countries to establish stable democratic institutions.

Nigeria

The arrival of Methodist missionaries in the nineteenth century led to the establishment of a modern education system.

Universities such as Ibadan and Nsukka developed under significant Christian influence.

Today, Nigeria stands as Africa's leading economy, in part due to the training of professionals and entrepreneurs that began in the colonial era.

South Africa

Missions of the Reformed Church founded some of the continent's most notable schools and universities.

Stellenbosch University and the University of Cape Town have missionary roots.

These institutions trained leaders who, after apartheid, helped transform the country.

Impact on Health and Social Well-Being

Christian missions played a crucial role in establishing the first modern hospitals and clinics in many African countries. The Christian principle of "serving one's neighbor" took shape through free medical care, vaccination campaigns, and nutrition programs.

For instance:

Kenya

Scottish missionaries founded the renowned Tenwek Hospital, which today remains an international referral center.

Uganda

Missionaries established hospitals and research centers that continue operating today.

Malawi

Cooperation between Christian missions and local governments significantly reduced infant mortality in several rural areas.

By improving public health, missionaries created a stronger foundation for economic development, since healthier populations are more productive and require less external support.

Botswana

Since the nineteenth century, Protestant missions have left a strong imprint on Botswana. After independence in 1966, the country built transparent and predictable institutions. Although Botswana's economy is driven mainly by diamonds, it has managed its resources with relative prudence, grounded in a civic culture marked by moderation. In this context, churches have played an important role by contributing to education, health, and the promotion of public integrity.

The country stands out for having one of the lowest corruption rates on the continent and for strong performance in community health programs and technical training.

Main mechanisms:

- Standards of honesty and public service.
- Sustainable social investment with church participation.
- Social capital that promotes collaboration among the state, businesses, and communities.

Rwanda

After 1994, Rwanda focused on reconstruction with an emphasis on social cohesion, fiscal discipline, and fighting corruption. In this context, churches and Christian organizations played an important role by collaborating in areas such as health, education, and reconciliation. They provided psychosocial support, job training, and promoted local productive projects.

As a result, public services have improved along with the regulatory environment and an emerging business climate, boosting growth in agribusiness, services, and technology.

Notable mechanisms:

- Church networks that foster trust and cooperation.
- Health and education programs that increase productivity.
- Work ethic and reconciliation as the basis of stability.

Latin America: Challenges and Hope

Throughout history, Latin America has faced numerous labor challenges, such as informality, labor exploitation, low wages, structural unemployment, and a lack of fair labor policies. Despite these persistent difficulties, there have been contexts in which Christianity acted as a driver of change.

Chile: Several Christian-inspired agricultural cooperatives have revitalized impoverished rural communities by turning them into sustainable economies through teaching stewardship principles and collective work.

Colombia: Groups like Christians for Peace have set up carpentry, sewing, and agriculture workshops for ex-combatants, showing that reconciliation can also be achieved through dignified work.

Haiti: The road ahead is long and complex. Factors such as the country's idiosyncrasies, negative influences from segments of the political elite, high illiteracy rates, and teachings from some Christian leaders, sometimes distorted or incomplete, have limited the Gospel's impact on the country's social and economic development. In addition, many people lack accurate information about what it truly means to be Christian and misinterpret their role in relation to economic and social progress. The absence of national leadership committed to living by biblical principles in public life has left the country without clear role models to translate these values into sustainable structural change.

The Effect on a Country's Culture

When a nation fosters a work ethic based on Christian principles, the result is not only increased productivity but also:

- Reduced administrative corruption.
- Higher levels of institutional trust.
- Lower violence and less destructive idleness.
- Promotion of gender equality and social entrepreneurship.
- Stronger family and community unity.

Work stops being oppressive and becomes a tool for personal and collective development.

Conclusion

Work should not lead to exhaustion but should be a source of purpose and personal growth. Christianity teaches that human beings were created to produce, collaborate, build, and serve. Nations that integrate this vocational sense into their work culture are better prepared to grow with justice, equity, and stability.

Investing in a Christian work ethic is a commitment to the soul of a country. A prosperous economy arises primarily from hearts and hands committed to working with excellence, integrity, and purpose.

These experiences show that when work is viewed as a vocation rather than a punishment, healthy communities, more stable local economies, and more equitable societies emerge.

CHAPTER TWO

Justice, Mercy, and Public Policy: A Call for Human-Centered Governance

A NATION'S SUCCESS is not based only on economic strength or military power. It rests on the justice that governs its institutions and on how compassionately it treats its most vulnerable citizens. In Scripture, God is presented not only as judge but also as defender of the orphan, protector of the foreigner, and redeemer of the poor. As Micah 6:8 says:

Here is a rewritten version: "O man, he has shown you what is good. And what does the Lord require of you? Only to do justice, to love mercy, and to walk humbly with your God."

This triad of justice, mercy, and humility provides a solid foundation for reframing public policy from an ethical, Christian perspective. Instead of focusing on the pursuit of power for its own sake or on impersonal economic growth, countries can adopt policy frameworks that harmonize legal order with practical compassion.

What does justice mean from a Christian perspective?

Justice in Scripture is neither abstract nor strictly legalistic. It demands concrete actions that promote the common good and protect the most vulnerable. As Psalm 82:3 states:

"Protect the weak and the fatherless; do justice for the afflicted and the needy."

In short, a just society does not only punish wrongdoing. It also prevents structural suffering, secures opportunity, and treats all citizens equitably.

Applied to public policy, this implies:

- Equitable access to education.
- Quality healthcare for all.
- Transparency in government.
- A legal system that is accessible and free of corruption.
- Labor protections for vulnerable people.

And what does mercy mean in the political sphere?

Mercy is not a sign of weakness, but of strength directed toward others. In situations of poverty, violence, or social exclusion, public policy should function as a healing tool. Like the Good Samaritan in the parable of the Gospel of Luke (10:25–37), the state must go beyond rhetoric and become an active agent of help, restoration, and steady support.

Compassionate policies are not spontaneous acts of charity, but organized structures that:

- Restore the dignity of those who have fallen.

- Accompany single mothers, displaced people, and those struggling with addictions.
- Reintegrate ex-offenders and war veterans.
- Protect children who have no family.
- Provide support to the elderly, people with disabilities, and victims of violence.

Examples from the Past and Present

In Costa Rica, the marked influence of Christian thought on its constitution and education system helped form a culture of peace, public health, and literacy that today places the country among the most stable in Latin America. The decision to abolish the military in 1949 was based on principles of pacification and equity.

In Haiti, several Christian organizations have advocated for reform of the judicial and education systems with a focus on community justice and human development. These initiatives aim to challenge elitist colonial models that have historically excluded the economically disadvantaged majority.

In the Dominican Republic, initiatives led by churches and Christian NGOs have worked alongside the state to eradicate child labor, rehabilitate young people in conflict with the law, and prevent domestic violence. These actions seek to promote public policies grounded in biblical values.

Justice and Compassion in Global Policies

Even in international contexts, countries with strong Christian roots have shown a tendency to promote welfare systems. A clear example is the Nordic nations, which, although more secular today, have moral foundations rooted in Christian principles related to human dignity, fair work, and social responsibility.

A Challenge for Nations: Elevate Ethics in Politics Without Mixing It with Religious Belief

One current challenge is that when Christianity is discussed in the political sphere, many mistake it for fanaticism or religious imposition. However, an active faith in public life does not aim to control. It aims to serve. As Jesus taught:

"Whoever wants to be first among you must become your servant." (Matthew 20:27)

Therefore, the goal is not to force the Christianization of governments, but to infuse institutions with eternal principles such as love, justice, compassion, and truth.

Conclusion

When public policies are grounded in justice and compassion, a nation prospers. Christianity provides solid, universal principles that can transform governments without turning into religious authoritarianism. True Christian leadership does not impose religious laws; it builds bridges, protects the vulnerable, and acts with integrity.

In the pages ahead, we will examine how these values are applied specifically in education with Christian foundations, cultivating not only well-informed citizens but also people of integrity devoted to serving their nation.

CHAPTER THREE

Education Based on Christian Values: Forging Character for the Country's Progress

EDUCATION IS ONE OF THE most powerful tools to change a society. However, not every form of instruction leads to positive change. Intellectual training without a moral foundation can produce brilliant yet corrupt people and competent yet self-serving leaders. In this context, education grounded in Christian values presents an essential alternative: forming whole individuals with knowledge, ethical awareness, and a vocation for service.

From ancient times, the Bible has treated teaching as a sacred duty. In Deuteronomy 6:6-7, we read:

"These words that I command you today shall be on your heart. You shall repeat them to your children and speak of them when you are at home, when you walk along the road, when you lie down, and when you get up."

This passage shows that Christian education is not merely an academic task. It is an ongoing process of transmitting principles and values that shape both behavior and the future of generations.

What do Christian values mean in education?

Christian values in education do not imply religious indoctrination. They promote universal principles that contribute to society's well-being. These include:

- Truth and honesty in the intellectual sphere
- Respect for others and for authority
- Individual and community responsibility
- Solidarity, service, and humility

Justice, Compassion, and Empathy

By integrating these values into school or university curricula, students not only develop thinking skills but also learn to live with integrity. This strengthens the social fabric, reduces corruption, improves coexistence, and forms citizens committed to the common good.

Social and Economic Impact of Value-Based Education

Improves culture in the workplace and civic sphere.

Students educated in values tend to become honest, law-abiding, responsible, and fair workers. This not only boosts productivity but also lowers social costs related to crime and fraud.

Promotes Ethical Entrepreneurship

Education focused on purpose and service motivates many young people to launch projects that generate social impact as well as economic benefits.

Fosters Equality and Values Diversity

The Christian principle that we are all created in the image of God (Genesis 1:27) undergirds respect for human dignity and is essential for an inclusive society.

Historical and Contemporary Cases

- **Nineteenth century (Chile and Argentina):** Numerous Christian missionaries established some of the first rural schools and hospitals. These efforts not only advanced literacy but also instilled values of dignity, service, and work.
- **Dominican Republic:** Institutions such as UNIBE and PUCMM have promoted educational projects that incorporate training in ethics and citizenship.
- **Colombia:** Organizations like Fe y Alegría have helped transform communities through educational programs in areas affected by violence.
- **Haiti:** Christian educational institutions have provided opportunities where the state system has not. For example, the Eben-Ezer Mission school network offers free education with a strong emphasis on spiritual formation, leadership, and community responsibility.

Jesus Christ as an Example in Education

Jesus was an extraordinary teacher. His approach combined deep knowledge, empathy, moral firmness, and a strong capacity to adapt. He taught in synagogues, on the streets, in homes, and in the countryside. He used parables, questions, and practical experiences to convey his lessons. His method was transformative because it reached not only the mind but also the heart of his listeners.

In Luke 2:52, we read:

"And Jesus grew in wisdom and stature, and in favor with God and people."

This verse captures a holistic education: intellectual growth (wisdom), physical development (stature), spiritual formation (favor with God), and social maturity (favor with others).

The Role of the Family, the Church, and the State in Transformative Education

A truly transformative education cannot depend on a single institution. It requires coordinated and complementary involvement from three essential pillars: the family, the church, and the state. Each one plays a specific and irreplaceable role in the integral development of the human person and, therefore, in building a prosperous and equitable society.

1. The Family: Foundation of Values, Driver of Development, and Pillar of National Prosperity

The family is the essential core of any society. At home, children receive their first lessons in love, respect, responsibility, solidarity, and faith before they ever attend school. It is in the home that values are instilled, character is formed, moral awareness is developed, and people are prepared to face life's challenges.

Sacred Scripture confirms this:

Here is a rewritten version: "Guide the child on the right path, and even when he is older, he will not depart from it."

Proverbs 22:6

A country's socioeconomic progress does not begin in parliaments, universities, or financial markets. It begins within the home. There arise the values that shape how we think, work together, and build prosperous and sustainable communities.

The Family as the First School of Values

The home is the first educational environment and the foundation on which all future learning is built. From their earliest years, children learn from their parents through direct teaching and, above all, by example. Among these are essential principles such as:

- Honesty → learning to tell the truth at all times.
- Respect → valuing one's own dignity and that of others.
- Responsibility means fulfilling both personal and social commitments.

- Discipline means developing habits of order, dedication, and perseverance.
- Solidarity means caring for others and working together.
- Faith and hope become trusting in God and maintaining a forward-looking vision.

A family that embraces and shares these values helps form individuals who are emotionally stable, ethically upright, and socially responsible. These are essential elements for building strong and resilient societies.

The Influence of Christian Principles on the Family

Christianity offers a unique, transformative view of the family, seeing it as a divine design and a setting of sacrificial love. According to biblical teaching, the home should be a place where God is honored and where principles that strengthen life together are practiced.

"And above all, clothe yourselves with love, which is the perfect bond."

"Unless the Lord builds the house, the builders labor in vain." (Psalm 127:1)

When Christian families put faith, prayer, biblical teaching, and the example of daily life first, they shape individuals with a transcendent outlook and an ethical sense of service that influences both personal development and the social and economic spheres.

United Family, Successful Nation

Current studies and historical examples show that societies with strong families tend to achieve greater political stability, social cohesion, and economic prosperity. In countries where households transmit clear values and promote holistic education, the following are commonly observed:

Significant Increases in Investment in Human Capital

Families that prioritize education and lifelong learning motivate their children to reach higher levels of knowledge and skills, which strengthens national productivity.

Reduction in Inequality and Violence

Stable households provide emotional and moral guidance, lowering rates of crime, substance abuse, early pregnancies, and other social problems that hinder development.

Greater Sustainable Economic Development

When values such as discipline, honesty, teamwork, and financial responsibility are learned at home, they shape productive workers, upright entrepreneurs, and engaged citizens. This, in turn, drives both the economy and innovation.

The Consequences of Dysfunctional Families

Conversely, when the educational and moral role of the family weakens, the repercussions for society are significant:

- Increased social conflict and community divisions.
- More corruption and a lack of professional ethics.
- Greater dependence on public assistance systems.
- Reduced economic competitiveness and human capital.

Family Breakdown Limits National Potential

The breakdown of the family produces individuals with less emotional stability, less discipline, and reduced capacity for resilience, which limits a country's collective potential. This shows that no economic policy will be sufficient without a solid foundation of values beginning in the home.

The Christian Family as a Driver of Social Transformation

Christian families play a crucial role in rebuilding and strengthening society. Their mission goes beyond instilling values within the home; they are called to be transformative agents in their communities. By living out their faith, serving their neighbors, and practicing solidarity, they help build robust social networks and promote the development of more just communities.

Religious programs that include family counseling, support for education, emotional well-being, and encouragement of entrepreneurship have shown that faith can be a powerful resource for combating poverty and fostering collective progress.

Strategies to Strengthen the Role of the Family

For the family to fulfill its formative role effectively and contribute to socioeconomic development, it is essential to:

- Teach Christian values from childhood.
- Foster communication and a spirit of unity in the family to prevent conflict.
- Strengthen the role of parents as first educators and role models.

- Bring together church, school, and community to create a learning and support environment.
- Develop public policies that safeguard family unity and promote its economic stability.

Conclusion

The family is not only a group of people connected by blood. It is the fundamental core of society and the place where the future of nations is shaped. The strength of the home is essential because without it, economies can falter, institutions can lose cohesion, and values can erode. Christianity, by placing God at the center of family life, offers a solid foundation for forming responsible individuals, upright leaders, and devoted citizens. When families embrace the principles of the Gospel, they not only transform individual lives, they also plant the seeds for nations that are prosperous, just, and sustainable.

"My family and I will serve the Lord."

(Joshua 24:15)

2. The Church: Community of Faith, School of Principles, and Catalyst for Social Change

The church, understood as a community of faith, goes far beyond being merely a place to gather or a space dedicated to worship. It is a living institution with the mission of forming hearts, shaping consciences, and providing a moral and spiritual framework that guides both personal and collective decisions. In the midst of today's uncertainty, inequality, and social crises, the church stands as a solid source of principles that offer direction, hope, and meaning in individual lives.

The apostle Paul put it clearly:

"The church of the living God is the pillar and foundation of the truth."

(1 Timothy 3:15)

Therefore, the church not only safeguards the faith, but it also acts as a school of life. Its mission is to educate, guide, and serve by forming people of integrity and communities devoted to the common good.

The Church as an Educational Institution of Ethical Principles

Beyond its spiritual mission, the church plays a fundamental role as a school that teaches Christian values and ethics. Through biblical instruction, it promotes virtues such as:

- Honesty and transparency → maintaining integrity in both personal and professional life.
- Compassion and empathy: recognizing the dignity of every person and protecting the most vulnerable.
- Social responsibility means understanding that every personal choice affects the community.
- Justice and equity → fostering relationships grounded in respect and dignity.
- Service to one's neighbor means approaching every vocation as an opportunity to contribute to the well-being of the community.

These principles strengthen believers' character and form citizens with a solid ethic, capable of making decisions that benefit not only their own interests but also the country's social and economic well-being.

The Church: A Response in Times of Crisis

In situations where the social fabric has been compromised by corruption, violence, extreme poverty, or structural injustices, the church can serve as a beacon of hope and a crucial agent of change.

Prophetic witness: Raises its voice against oppressive systems, advocating for transparency and social justice.

Spaces for reconciliation: Promotes forgiveness and restoration in communities fractured by political, religious, or ethnic conflict.

Holistic care: Coordinates humanitarian actions, food distribution, medical services, and job-reintegration programs for vulnerable populations.

Education and technical training: Many congregations create schools, universities, and training centers that help develop human capital.

In this way, the church goes beyond the spiritual and becomes a key actor in rebuilding the social fabric. It guides communities to adopt models of coexistence grounded in dignity, solidarity, and mutual respect.

Consistency Between Teaching and Practice

The church's effectiveness as an agent of change is tied to its moral credibility. Preaching values is not enough; they must be embodied in daily life. When religious doctrine is paired with tangible actions oriented toward service, justice, and compassion, the church becomes a living model for the whole community.

A church that acts consistently builds trust and attracts those seeking a clear ethical example. However, if there is a gap between what is preached and what is practiced, the community loses influence and relevance in public life.

“Let your light shine before others, so that they may see your good works and glorify your Father in heaven.”

(Matthew 5:16)

The church’s credibility rests on its ability to serve as an example, beginning with personal transformation and, through it, changing the institutions and systems that make up society.

The Church as a Promoter of Transformative Vocations

One of the church’s most impactful contributions is its ability to give meaning to work and professional vocation. Christian teaching reframes the traditional concept of success. It is not merely about accumulating wealth. It is about serving with a clear purpose.

Believers begin to view their profession, whether in agriculture, business, medicine, politics, education, or the arts, as an opportunity to honor God and contribute to the well-being of the entire community. This perspective changes how they understand their role in society and drives:

Professional ethics: making the right decisions, even when they are not the easiest.

Responsible innovation: using God-given talents to create positive impact.

Leading with purpose: guiding teams and organizations toward goals that benefit everyone.

In this way, the church helps form people of integrity, dedicated workers, and influential leaders who become pillars of sustainable development.

Social and Economic Impact of the Church as an Institution

The church's influence goes beyond the spiritual. Its doctrines have a tangible impact on national development.

Mass education: Christian missions have traditionally established schools and universities that have educated generations of leaders, scientists, entrepreneurs, and public servants.

Reducing inequalities: The church promotes solidarity through social support programs, scholarships, and community networks that enable economic mobility.

Health and well-being: From founding hospitals to running preventive campaigns, the church has played a key role in building comprehensive healthcare systems.

Ethics and governance: Leaders formed in Christian values tend to prioritize the common good, creating environments of trust that attract investment and provide economic stability.

These contributions make the church a strategic ally for development, not only shaping individual character but also strengthening institutions and promoting more prosperous societies.

Church and Social Reconciliation

In communities marked by divisions, conflict, or historical wounds, the church has the potential to act as mediator and healer. By fostering forgiveness, unity, and mutual respect, it becomes a catalyst for national reconciliation processes.

Examples such as the involvement of Christian leaders in South Africa's democratic transition, including figures like Archbishop Desmond Tutu and the Truth and Reconciliation Commission, show that faith can serve as a powerful instrument for rebuilding divided communities.

Conclusion

The church is not only a religious institution. It is also a community of faith, a place where ethical principles are taught, and a catalyst for social and economic transformation. Its mission goes beyond simply preaching. It seeks to be a living testimony of service, justice, compassion, and hope.

When the church aligns its teaching with its practice, it becomes a guiding light for nations, shaping people of integrity, responsible leaders, and united communities. In a world full of complex challenges, it remains a driving force that motivates people to live with purpose and contribute to the common good.

"You are the light of the world. A city set on a hill cannot be hidden."

(Matthew 5:14)

3. The State: Guardian of Rights, Driver of the Common Good, and Strategic Ally in the Development of Nations

The State is a political entity whose legitimate purpose is to safeguard citizens' fundamental rights and ensure the common good. Its role is not limited to making laws or managing resources. It also includes creating dignified, fair, and equitable conditions that allow each person to fully develop their individual potential.

One of the State's most important responsibilities is to guarantee everyone access to complete, high-quality, and affordable education. This goes beyond simply building schools or awarding scholarships. It means creating inclusive public policies that promote equal opportunity, protect children, and strengthen human growth in all its dimensions, academic, social, emotional, moral, and spiritual.

When the State genuinely assumes this commitment, education stops being seen as a budget expense and is recognized as a strategic investment in the country's future. It is essential for competitiveness, social justice, and long-term sustainability.

Government and Education: An Investment in Human Capital

The economic and social growth of a nation is closely tied to its human capital, that is, the training, knowledge, and skills of its citizens. In this sense, education becomes a highly effective tool to combat poverty, reduce inequality, and drive innovation.

A government dedicated to education makes responsible investments in:

- Educational infrastructure: developing modern, accessible, and safe facilities.
- Programs and scholarships: providing support so that students, regardless of their economic situation, can reach a high level of education.
- High-quality teacher training: preparing teachers to become agents of change.
- Equity policies: ensuring that vulnerable sectors, minorities, and rural areas enjoy the same opportunities as the rest of the population.
- Holistic education: promoting not only academic skills but also critical thinking, civic awareness, and social responsibility.

State, Family, and Church: A Strategic Alliance

- The full development of a person and a country cannot depend on a single institution. It requires harmonious collaboration among three essential pillars: the family, the church, and the State.

- The family is the first educational environment where fundamental values such as respect, honesty, discipline, and solidarity are instilled.
- The church functions as an ethical and spiritual school, promoting values of justice, compassion, and service to one's neighbor.
- The State, in turn, is obligated to ensure just, inclusive, and equitable conditions that allow all citizens to reach their full development.

When these three actors work together in harmony, the results are notable:

- People are educated with firm values and professional skills.
- The social fabric is strengthened through cooperation and shared responsibility.
- Sustainable models of economic development, innovation, and social justice are created.

On the other hand, if any of these pillars fails to fulfill its role or neglects it, both the educational and social systems are harmed. When the family does not instill values, the church lacks coherence, or the State fails to provide equal opportunity, the chances of achieving significant social change decrease considerably.

The State's Obligation in Creating Collective Well-Being

The common good goes beyond personal interests and involves creating collective conditions that promote the integral development of all citizens. In this context, the State performs strategic functions:

- Ensure social justice by implementing policies that reduce inequalities and expand opportunities for the entire population.
- Protect fundamental rights, guaranteeing human dignity, freedom of worship, freedom of thought, and legal equality.
- Foster peace and security in society, establishing environments that encourage harmonious and effective coexistence.
- Promote research and innovation through investment in science, technology, and new models of economic development.

Education, Ethics, and Active Civic Participation

The State has the responsibility not only to ensure that citizens acquire academic knowledge, but also to promote an education that forms ethical, critical individuals who are committed to their community.

This requires an education strategy that incorporates:

Critical thinking: instruction in analysis, evaluation, and constructive questioning.

Civics: educating responsible, informed, and active citizens.

Social responsibility: forming leaders who view their work and skills as a service to the common good.

By fostering these values, the State helps reduce corruption, strengthen institutions, and create a virtuous circle in which quality education drives economic prosperity and social stability.

Joining Forces for National Change

The real progress of a society is not based solely on legal reforms or isolated government programs. Full development occurs when the family, the church, and the State collaborate with shared responsibility, forming people of integrity who are socially responsible and focused on the common good.

When the values instilled in the family, the principles promoted by the church, and the opportunities guaranteed by the State work together in harmony, the result is:

- Reduced poverty through education and dignified employment.
- Greater social cohesion through respect, empathy, and cooperation.
- Institutional stability is achieved through more aware and engaged citizens.
- Sustainable economic growth based on innovation and productivity.
- However, if any one of these three actors abandons its mission, the expectation of change diminishes. Progress requires shared responsibility and a common vision.

Conclusion

When the State acts with legitimacy and commitment, it becomes a strategic ally for building just, educated, and prosperous societies. Its role as guarantor of rights and promoter of the common good is irreplaceable. Its impact increases significantly when it works in partnership with the family and the church.

True development is not achieved through the isolated action of a single institution. It is achieved when all social actors assume their shared responsibility to form citizens with solid values, social awareness, and a commitment to the common good.

"Righteousness exalts a nation, but sin is a disgrace to any people."

(Proverbs 14:34)

The Role of the Family, the Church, and the State in Transformative Education: The Case of Haiti

An education that truly transforms depends on the coordinated action of three fundamental pillars: the family, the church, and the State. When these work in harmony, a more stable, productive, and equitable society emerges. However, in contexts like Haiti, where one or more of these pillars are fragile or do not fulfill their functions properly, a vicious cycle appears, marked by persistent poverty, lack of information, and social distrust.

The Family: The First School of Values

In Haiti, many families face severe economic challenges, migration pressures, and a lack of access to adequate basic education. This often results in parents being absent physically and emotionally, leaving children to grow up without continuous guidance. When the home does not instill fundamental values such as discipline, respect, honesty, and responsibility, young people face a greater risk of succumbing to destructive ideologies or adopting regressive social practices. Without a strong family core, it is difficult to expect any other institution to adequately compensate for the absence of basic moral formation and affection.

The Church: Community of Faith and School of Ethical Principles

In Haiti, many churches have a significant presence, yet not all consistently fulfill their transformative role. Some religious communities have failed to form leaders dedicated to social justice and national development. Instead, they have spread incomplete or distorted teachings about Christianity that reduce religion to emotional comfort disconnected from civic and economic responsibilities. This misinformation has led many believers to view their faith as something separate from material and social advancement. A genuinely committed church should teach that biblical principles include dignified work, responsible stewardship of resources, and the active pursuit of the common good.

The State as Guarantor of Rights and Promoter of the Common Good

In Haiti, the State has failed in its responsibility to ensure universal, dignified, quality education. Corruption, lack of leadership, and the inability to enforce laws have greatly weakened educational institutions. In addition, the absence of a national leader who embodies and promotes Christian principles in public life has contributed to a lack of inspiring models that build trust and drive coordinated efforts toward national development. Without clear and effective policies, the gap between rich and poor widens, illiteracy persists, and formal job opportunities remain limited.

When the three pillars work in harmony, Haiti's reconstruction cannot depend solely on humanitarian aid or external investment. It is essential for families to restore their role as the primary shapers of fundamental values, for the church to promote and exemplify Christian principles that are relevant to the economic and social spheres, and for the State to ensure favorable conditions along with accessible policies that offer everyone a transformative education. When these three elements effectively fulfill their roles, it becomes possible to break the cycle of poverty and begin a genuine path toward sustainable progress. Otherwise, any change achieved will be merely superficial and short-lived.

Conclusion

A nation with education but without values lacks a soul. However, by investing in education grounded in Christian principles, you form not only workers or professionals but also agents of change, just leaders, responsible parents, and committed citizens.

The future of a nation is forged in its classrooms. Therefore, the values transmitted there will significantly shape the social and economic well-being of future generations. Choosing an education based on Christian principles is to sow justice, hope, and stability for tomorrow.

CHAPTER FOUR

Economy Grounded in Biblical Principles: Justice, Equity, and Sustainable Prosperity

ONE OF THE MOST frequent misconceptions about the Bible is to assume that its teachings are limited only to the spiritual and moral sphere. However, Scripture is filled with economic principles that have guided responsible resource management, promoted social justice, fostered ethical commerce, and helped combat poverty. Over time, nations that have incorporated these values, even if not always perfectly, have seen increases in stability, economic growth, and collective well-being.

In Deuteronomy 8:18, we read:

"Remember the Lord your God, for it is he who grants you the power to generate wealth, in order to confirm his covenant."

Fundamental Biblical Economic Principles

The Bible not only provides spiritual principles for individual salvation. It also sets clear guidelines for a nation's economic and social order. Applied consistently, these guidelines promote justice, sustainable prosperity, and community stability.

1. Honest and Dedicated Work as a Means to Economic Prosperity

"The strategies of the diligent certainly lead to abundance, but the one who rushes without thinking will surely end in poverty."

From the biblical perspective, work is not a curse. It is a vocation and a blessing. God placed the human being in the Garden of Eden "to cultivate it and care for it" (Genesis 2:15), indicating that productive effort is part of the original design.

The value of work: the legitimate way to acquire resources, develop skills, and contribute to the well-being of the community.

Planning and perseverance: abundance does not come through shortcuts or impulses. It comes through disciplined processes that include saving, investing, and responsible management.

Social implication: A society that promotes an ethic of honest work produces self-sufficient citizens and reduces dependence on external aid.

2. Prohibition of Fraud and Corruption

"The Lord detests dishonest scales but delights in accurate weights."

Scripture condemns every form of deceit in economic transactions. The metaphor of the "false balance" represents any unjust system that distorts the true value of goods to obtain undue gain.

Fair trade: transparent pricing, proper conduct, and respect for established agreements.

Transparency and trust: corruption harms the economy by eroding trust, an essential component of exchange and investment.

National impact: where corruption is systemic, resources concentrate in the hands of a privileged few, leaving the majority without access to the benefits of development.

3. Equitable Distribution and Provision for Those in Need

"Whoever has two tunics should share with the one who has none, and whoever has food should do the same."

The biblical system included specific mechanisms to prevent excessive wealth concentration and to ensure that the most vulnerable had access to essentials:

The tithe: beyond its spiritual meaning, it supported religious leadership and provided assistance to orphans, widows, and foreigners (Deuteronomy 14:28–29).

The sabbatical year: every seven years, the land rested and debts were canceled, offering economic relief to the disadvantaged (Exodus 23:10–11; Deuteronomy 15:1–2).

The Jubilee: every fifty years, properties that had been sold returned to their original owners, preventing permanent land concentration (Leviticus 25:10).

These principles did not promote passive assistance. They established a balanced system that protected the dignity of those in need and prevented extreme inequality.

4. Ban on Exploitative Labor

"Do not exploit the poor and needy worker."

Workers, especially those in vulnerable situations, must receive dignified treatment and fair compensation.

Prompt payment: Biblical law required wages to be paid the same day, since many lived day to day and depended on those earnings for food (Leviticus 19:13).

Sabbath rest: intended not only for workers but also for work animals (Exodus 20:8-11), recognizing rest as essential to human productivity.

Ethical responsibility of employers: economic power must be used for the collective good, not to take advantage of those in need.

Application for National Progress

1) Honest and Diligent Work as a Source of Wealth

Diagnosis: High levels of informality, low productivity, forced migration, and a mismatch between educational training and labor market demands.

Actions: Family/Community: Vocational schools in neighborhoods (3–6 months) offering training in carpentry, masonry, agro-processing, solar energy, sewing, and mobile repair. Includes supervised internships with local micro-contracts.

Church: "Work and Calling" programs (theology of work + soft skills development like punctuality, customer service, personal finances, and saving 10–20%).

State/Alliances: "Dual training" zones (company–workshop–school) offering tax incentives for each apprentice certified and employed for 12 months or more.

Solidarity Finance: Rotating savings and micro-credit with mentoring (providing not just money but also advice on costs and sales).

Indicators: Employment placement at 6 and 12 months after training; microenterprise formalization rate; productivity by occupation; average savings per household.

2) Prohibition of Fraud and Corruption ("Just Balance")

Diagnosis: Systemic corruption undermines trust and increases transaction costs.

Actions: Church and Civil Society: Agreements on honesty within congregations and the business realm (public regulations, mutual audits, reporting system).

State: A single portal for public procurement with open data, electronic bidding, and full process tracking (from tender to award, delivery, and payment).

Education: Applied ethics modules in schools and vocational training (invoicing, measurements, warranties; practice of "fair price").

Sanctions and Exemplary Model: Effective suspension for fraud, along with public case disclosures; annual recognition of "Fair Balance Companies."

Key Indicators: Percentage of procurement processes using open data; average time for supplier payments; investigated and sanctioned reports; citizen trust surveys.

3) Equitable Distribution and Provision for the Needy (Through Tithe, Sabbatical Year, and Jubilee)

Diagnosis: Persistent disparity and instability; unpaid debts; unproductive assets.

Church: Mercy funds with defined norms (food, basic healthcare, education) and productive opportunities (initial capital + mentorship).

State: Debt relief programs for micro-producers conditioned on participating in training and presenting a business plan; incentives for hiring young people and women.

Land and Assets (Spirit of Jubilee): A bank for unused land for social leasing; agricultural cooperatives with guaranteed sales to the public sector (e.g., school breakfast programs).

Social Sabbatical: Temporary suspension of obligations in disaster-affected areas, along with technical assistance to restart activities.

Indicators: Number of households rising above extreme poverty; microcredits with effective payment rates; cultivated land under associative models; school enrollment and retention rates.

4) Prohibition of Labor Exploitation (Fair Wages and Adequate Rest Time)

Diagnosis: Inconsistent wages, delayed payments, and lack of job security.

Actions: Basic Framework: Simplified one-page contracts (hours, pay, safety), digital receipts through mobile, and a bi-weekly payment calendar.

Church/Faith-based Companies: "Dignified Employment" certification (timely payment, personal protective equipment, day off, safe environments for women and youth).

Smart Inspection: Anonymous hotline, random visits with public checklists, proportional penalties, and corrective training.

Indicators: Compliance with payment deadlines; workplace accident incidence; staff turnover rate; percentage of properly documented contracts.

Governance and Culture: How to Make It Work?

Local integrity and development councils (family-church-business-state) that implement annual plans, set goals, and generate quarterly reports.

Character development: Curricula for primary, secondary, and vocational education that promote habits of diligence, truthfulness, service, and citizenship.

Exemplary leadership: Pastors, entrepreneurs, and authorities publicly disclose their declarations of interests and budgets to "lead with transparency."

National Transformation Metrics (Macro)

Increase in formal employment, growth in sectoral productivity, reduction in extreme poverty, improvement in institutional trust, rise in public integrity scores, and decrease in school dropout rates.

Main Message

Biblical ethics is not merely a devotional ornament; it establishes incentives, regulates power, and ennobles work. In Haiti, aligning culture (represented by the family), principles (promoted by the church), and institutions (led by the state) with these four pillars has the potential to break the cycle of poverty and lay the foundation for genuine shared prosperity.

A People-Centered Economy

Contemporary economics, particularly in its most neoliberal form, tends to reduce people to mere numbers. In contrast, Christianity teaches that the economy should be oriented toward human well-being, not the other way around. This means:

- Setting restrictions on financial speculation that negatively impact the most disadvantaged.
- Ensuring fair compensation.
- Fostering access to property, credit, and entrepreneurship in marginalized sectors.
- Promoting a culture of saving, responsibility, and generosity.

Jesus Christ and the Prudent Management of Resources

Jesus taught more about money than about heaven and hell combined—not because he valued material things over the spiritual, but because he understood that the economy reflects the essence of the human heart. In the parable of the faithful steward (Luke 16:10), he says:

"He who is faithful in little things will also be faithful in much."

Jesus valued generosity, as seen in the story of the widow who gave all she had. However, he also condemned attitudes such as greed, avarice, and the love of money (Luke 12:15). For him, wealth was a tool meant to be used with a righteous purpose.

Implications for National Economic Policy

An economy grounded in biblical principles is not about imposing religious laws, but fostering a development ethic that promotes justice. This involves:

- Developing national budgets with a people-centered perspective.
- Eliminating fiscal benefits for corrupt elites.
- Investing in education, healthcare, and employment access.
- Supporting small producers and committed entrepreneurs.
- Safeguarding natural resources is part of our responsibility for environmental stewardship.

Conclusion

An economy devoid of values can be destructive. In contrast, one based on biblical principles has the power to transform. While the Bible does not offer magical solutions, it provides the foundation for a moral economy: one focused on people, guided by justice, driven by generosity, and committed to promoting equity.

For nations to achieve lasting prosperity, it is necessary to reevaluate the values that govern their markets, banks, businesses, and governments. Blessing is not inherited; it is built when eternal principles guide temporary decisions.

CHAPTER FIVE

Historical Cases of Christian Development: Faith in Action for the Common Good

THROUGHOUT THE CENTURIES, Christianity has demonstrated that the practical and consistent application of its principles can bring about significant transformations in entire communities, elevate societies, and drive sustainable development. While no country has perfectly implemented these principles, there are numerous examples where the influence of Christianity has been key to achieving significant economic and social progress.

This chapter highlights several of these cases, from the origins of the modern world to current experiences in Europe, the United States, Latin America, and the Caribbean.

Europe: The Rise of Modern Progress After the Reformation

One of the most analyzed examples is the effect of the 16th-century Protestant Reformation. Nations such as Switzerland, the Netherlands, Germany, and Scotland experienced profound changes due to a new perspective on faith, work, and individual responsibility. This transformation encompassed not only spiritual aspects but also educational, economic, and political dimensions.

The Reformation promoted universal literacy by establishing the need to learn to read in order to access the Bible. This led to significant educational reforms on a large scale.

The ethics of responsible work were promoted: work was considered a divine vocation ("calling"), which encouraged both productivity and honesty.

The concept of financial stewardship promoted savings, prudent investment, and fiscal responsibility, enabling the emergence of ethical banks and solid family-owned businesses.

This cultural shift helped the rise of modern capitalism, as Max Weber argues, and also strengthened democratic structures, making them more solid and participatory. The United States, Latin America, and the Caribbean.

The United States of America

In the United States, a prominent and significant example of how Christian faith impacted the country's social, political, and economic development is the Civil Rights Movement. Led during the 1950s and 1960s by Dr. Martin Luther King Jr., this movement was deeply inspired by biblical principles and Christian values to advocate for social justice, equal rights, and human dignity. Through his focus on peaceful and non-violent resistance, King promoted a major structural change.

The foundation of his leadership was rooted in the Gospel and the belief that "every person is created in the image of God" (Genesis 1:27). This principle guided the fight against racial segregation, discrimination, and social injustices. King viewed faith not only as an individual experience but also as a collective commitment to others and to the development of a more equitable society. For him, acting in favor of justice was a Christian mandate that transcended racial, cultural, and economic differences.

The Role of Christian Churches

African American churches were pivotal in the Civil Rights Movement, serving as spiritual and strategic centers for community organization, education, and resistance. These spaces were where marches were planned, legal support was provided, and the morale of participants was strengthened. Pastors and Christian leaders spread messages of unity, forgiveness, and perseverance, emphasizing that the fight should be carried out not with hatred but with love, as taught in the Sermon on the Mount: "Love your enemies and pray for those who persecute you" (Matthew 5:44).

Faith in action mobilized thousands of people, including not only African American communities but also white religious leaders and interdenominational organizations. These groups found a common cause in social justice grounded in the Gospel. The Christian dimension of the movement gave it unshakable moral strength, drawing national and international attention to the reality of racial segregation in the United States.

Impact of Legislation and Social Transformation

The fusion of Christian leadership, community mobilization, and peaceful resistance led to historic transformations. Two essential laws marked a before and after in American society:

- The Civil Rights Act of 1964: It eliminated discrimination in public spaces, employment, and government-funded programs, ensuring equal opportunities for all.
- The Voting Rights Act of 1965: It removed legal barriers that hindered African American communities from exercising their right to vote, thus strengthening democracy and promoting greater civic participation.

These advancements, deeply influenced by faith and Christian values, changed the country's social structure and laid the foundation for new generations that continue to fight for equity and human rights.

Christian Faith as a Driver of National Unity

This historical case shows that Christian faith, when practiced through concrete actions for the common good, can be a powerful tool for social and political transformation. The values of compassion, solidarity, justice, and reconciliation inspired leaders, communities, and organizations to work together despite deep racial divisions.

The influence of this movement went beyond the religious realm, impacting culture, education, and politics in the United States. Today, the legacy of Dr. King and the Christian churches that supported him continues to serve as a global example of how faith-based values can contribute to collective progress.

Historical Analysis of Christian Development: The Protestant Ethic and the Economic Rise of the United States

In addition to the social and political impact of Christianity, as reflected in the Civil Rights Movement, another crucial aspect of Christian development in the United States is the influence of Protestant ethics on the shaping of the national economic model.

Since the 17th century, when Puritan pilgrims arrived in North America seeking religious freedom, the Christian faith has had a profound influence on work culture, productivity, and social responsibility. These predominantly Protestant groups believed that work was not simply a means of earning a living, but a divine calling granted by God. Their purpose extended beyond accumulating personal wealth; they also sought to contribute to the collective well-being and promote community development.

The Beginning of the Protestant Work Ethic

The root of this mindset comes from the biblical interpretation of stewardship: humans are managers of the resources and talents that God has granted them. According to this principle, qualities such as discipline, organization, honesty, and effort are seen as expressions of faith. Doing work with excellence and responsibility was perceived as a form of worship to God.

The German sociologist Max Weber, in his work The Protestant Ethic and the Spirit of Capitalism (1905), notes that these ideas favored the emergence of an entrepreneurial and productive mindset in the American colonies. Austerity, savings, investment in education, and a rejection of idleness became fundamental values in this society, fostering a culture oriented towards self-sufficiency and collective progress.

Historical Impact on U.S. Society

During the 18th and 19th centuries, Christian values had a direct impact on the growth of the U.S. economy. Protestant communities encouraged mass education through schools and universities established by churches. They promoted technological innovation as well as the development of small and medium-sized businesses, firmly integrating the notion that achieving material prosperity should be accompanied by a moral responsibility towards others.

This model was the inspiration for fundamental principles such as:

- The entrepreneurial spirit is based on the freedom to take initiatives and continuous effort.
- Community responsibility means actively participating in social progress.
- Collaboration between different denominations, where several churches joined together to promote educational programs, hospitals, and social services.

Thanks to this perspective, the United States experienced steady economic growth, establishing itself as one of the most prosperous and influential nations in the world.

Christianity, Prosperity, and Collective Well-being

Although material prosperity was one of the most evident results of the Protestant ethic, the true impact of Christianity on the development of the United States lies in its emphasis on moral integrity, fairness, and social service. Various Christian leaders and churches dedicated their resources to community projects, missions, hospitals, and welfare programs, creating a network of social support that benefited millions of people.

This connection between faith, work, and the common good laid the foundation for a culture that values personal responsibility, education, innovation, and solidarity. Even today, numerous U.S. institutions, from universities to charitable organizations, maintain deep roots in the Christian principles that guided the early settlers and influenced the country's development.

Conclusion

Both the Civil Rights Movement, led by Martin Luther King Jr., and the Protestant ethic in the country's economic development represent two distinct but complementary aspects of Christian development in the United States. On one hand, faith drove a struggle for social justice; on the other hand, it served as a catalyst to foster prosperity and responsibility within communities.

These cases demonstrate that when Christian values, such as love for others, discipline, solidarity, and justice, are put into daily practice, they not only transform individual lives. They also bring about structural changes in an entire society by influencing its politics, economy, and culture.

A Historical Case of Christian Development: The Role of Christianity in the Abolition of Slavery in the United States

During the 18th and 19th centuries, slavery symbolized one of the greatest moral contradictions in the newly formed United States. Despite the founding principles of the country proclaiming liberty, equality, and human dignity, millions of African Americans endured inhuman conditions within a deeply entrenched system of slavery, particularly in the Southern states.

In response to this situation, Christian churches, along with religious leaders and activists motivated by their faith, played a crucial role in the abolitionist movement. Their conviction was grounded in the central idea of Christianity: all human beings are created in the image and likeness of God (Genesis 1:27). This made slavery incompatible with the biblical values of justice, dignity, and love for one's neighbor.

Abolitionism and Christianity

From the late 18th century, several Protestant congregations, especially Quakers, Methodists, Baptists, and Presbyterians, began publicly questioning the legitimacy of slavery. The Quakers were pioneers in creating anti-slavery societies and establishing networks to assist runaway slaves.

The message was clear: this was not merely a political or economic dilemma but also a moral and spiritual struggle. Drawing on passages like Galatians 3:28, "There is neither Jew nor Greek, slave nor free, male nor female; for you are all one in Christ Jesus," Christian abolitionists argued that slavery contradicted the core of the Gospel.

Leaders like William Lloyd Garrison and Harriet Beecher Stowe, author of Uncle Tom's Cabin, managed to mobilize thousands of people through speeches, literature, and national campaigns. These activities exposed the suffering of slaves and sparked a moral awakening in the conscience of the nation.

The Underground Railroad: Faith in Action

A prominent example of how Christian faith turned into concrete actions was the "Underground Railroad." This secret network consisted of routes, safe houses, and shelters that helped slaves escape to the free states in the North or Canada.

This underground system was primarily established by Christians dedicated to the principles of the Gospel, who risked their lives, property, and freedom to provide refuge, food, and guidance to fugitive individuals.

People like Harriet Tubman, nicknamed "Moses" for her leadership in these missions, led hundreds of slaves to freedom. Her inspiration came from an unwavering faith and a firm conviction that she was fulfilling a divine mandate.

The Legislative Effect and the End of the Conflict

The persistent effort of Christian movements and abolitionist leaders generated crucial social and political pressure to push for legislative changes. As a result, after the Civil War (1861–1865), a historic achievement was made with the ratification of the 13th Amendment to the U.S.

Constitution in 1865, which officially abolished slavery throughout the country.

The impact of Christianity was fundamental, not only in inspiring the struggle but also in providing a moral framework for the political decisions that led to the liberation of millions of people. This movement highlighted how faith can be a transformative force when combined with the principle of justice, challenging and altering deeply rooted social and political structures.

Legacy and Knowledge for Contemporary Society

The process of abolishing slavery in the United States illustrates how an active practice of Christianity, committed to human dignity and freedom, can lead to significant historical transformations. The principles of justice, equality, and love for one's neighbor became driving forces that overcame denominational, racial, and social barriers.

Today, this legacy continues to inspire contemporary movements working to eradicate inequalities, combat discrimination, and promote human rights. All of this is done under the same vision that every life holds immeasurable value in the eyes of God.

General Summary of the Three Cases

1. Through the Civil Rights Movement, Christian faith demonstrated its ability to overcome social barriers and advocate for equality.

2. With the Protestant Ethic, faith promoted both economic growth and a sense of responsibility toward the community.
3. With the Abolition of Slavery, faith became a driving force toward freedom, justice, and restoration.

These three examples show that Christian faith, when focused on the common good, has the power to bring about significant changes capable of transforming both individual lives and the entire destiny of a nation.

Latin America and the Caribbean: Examples of Transformation with Christian Roots

Throughout history, Latin America and the Caribbean have faced numerous complex challenges marked by armed conflicts, social inequalities, political tensions, and economic crises. In this context, Christianity has played a crucial role as an agent of social, spiritual, and community transformation. Catholic, evangelical churches, and interdenominational institutions have consistently strived to restore human dignity, promote social justice, and strengthen community bonds.

One of the most notable examples of this positive impact is found in Colombia, a country deeply affected by more than fifty years of internal armed conflict. The participation of Christian communities in reconciliation processes, peacebuilding, and social reconstruction clearly demonstrates how faith can be transformed into concrete actions for the common good.

Reconciliation and Peace in Colombia

In the process of demobilization and reintegration of former combatants in Colombia, particularly since the peace agreements signed in 2016 between the government and the Revolutionary Armed Forces of Colombia (FARC), various evangelical Christian churches and faith-based organizations played a crucial role.

In addition to offering spiritual support, these churches implemented comprehensive programs aimed at both former combatants and communities impacted by the conflict. Some of their most notable contributions include:

Spiritual and Moral Support: Through pastoral counseling, discipleship programs, and areas dedicated to emotional healing, many individuals discovered a new purpose in their lives, grounded in Christian values of forgiveness, restoration, and reconciliation.

Literacy and Basic Education Programs: Various churches promoted initiatives to combat illiteracy among former combatants, supporting them in completing their academic education and facilitating their integration into the workforce.

Job Training and Entrepreneurship: In collaboration with non-governmental organizations and the private sector, churches launched technical training workshops. These courses were designed to provide productive skills in various areas such as agriculture, carpentry, bakery, and technology.

Psychological Support and Emotional Recovery: Groups of psychologists and therapists, many affiliated with Christian ministries, worked to heal the trauma caused by violence and rebuild both self-esteem and trust in the civilian environment.

The Role of Faith in Establishing Peace

The most notable contribution of Christian communities in Colombia has been fostering a culture of peace. Based on biblical values, such as "Blessed are the peacemakers, for they will be called children of God" (Matthew 5:9), the churches have played a crucial role in redefining the concepts of forgiveness and reconciliation on both individual and collective levels.

Christian leaders urged victims to break the cycles of hatred and vengeance, also encouraging former combatants to take moral responsibility for their actions by rebuilding their lives based on principles of dignity and respect. In various rural areas, where the state's presence was limited, churches became safe havens for dialogue between victims, perpetrators, and local authorities. This facilitated restorative justice processes and promoted social cohesion.

Impact on Society and Community

The efforts of Christian churches in Colombia have produced concrete results:

- Reduction in Recidivism in Violent Acts: Former combatants who participated in Christian-based training and reintegration programs showed greater success in developing new, meaningful life projects.
- Empowerment of Vulnerable Communities: Reconciliation initiatives fostered peaceful relationships between groups that had historically been in conflict, creating spaces for cooperation and joint development.

- Creation of Solidarity Networks: Churches, NGOs, community leaders, and government entities established strategic alliances to comprehensively address the needs of affected populations.

Rural Development-Dominican Republic

In the Dominican Republic, Christianity has been crucial in transforming socially and economically disadvantaged rural communities. Through cooperation between international Christian organizations, such as World Vision and Visión Mundial, along with local churches, comprehensive projects have been implemented to improve the quality of life, strengthen community bonds, and foster sustainable development.

These organizations are based on the principles of compassion, justice, and service to others, values deeply embedded in the Christian message. Their primary mission is to provide practical solutions to urgent needs, combining humanitarian aid with community training to achieve sustainable impact.

Access to Clean Water and Basic Sanitation Services

One of the most notable advancements in rural communities in the Dominican Republic has been the establishment of potable water systems in areas where basic infrastructure was historically lacking. Thanks to strategic partnerships with local churches, community leaders, and municipal authorities, World Vision, alongside Visión Mundial, has carried out projects that include:

- Installation of hand-dug wells and pumping systems to ensure a constant supply of drinking water.
- Implementation of community distribution networks to supply families, schools, and health centers.
- Hygiene and sanitation training to reduce the risk of waterborne diseases, particularly among children and vulnerable populations.

These programs have significantly reduced the incidence of gastrointestinal diseases and improved public health indicators, demonstrating a direct and sustainable impact on the quality of life for thousands of families.

Sustainable Agriculture and Food Security

Poverty in rural areas of the Dominican Republic is deeply connected to the lack of access to advanced agricultural technologies and a dependence on traditional farming methods. To address this issue, various Christian organizations have launched programs focused on sustainable agriculture. These programs promote productive practices that are environmentally respectful and strengthen the economic resilience of local communities.

By introducing innovative farming techniques, providing access to resources such as high-quality seeds, tools, and training, these organizations help farmers improve crop yields while protecting the environment. The focus on sustainability ensures that farming methods remain viable over the long term, empowering communities to become more self-sufficient and reduce their vulnerability to economic and environmental shocks.

The most important initiatives are:

Technical Training for Farmers on Planting Techniques, Crop Rotation, and Efficient Soil Management:

- Providing farmers with hands-on education on sustainable farming methods to increase productivity and soil health.

Implementation of Drip Irrigation Systems and Water-Optimizing Technologies:

- Introducing water-efficient technologies, such as drip irrigation, to reduce water waste and improve crop yields.

Crop Diversification to Ensure Food Security and Reduce Dependency on Monocultures:

- Encouraging farmers to grow a variety of crops, reducing the risks associated with monoculture farming, and ensuring a more stable food supply.

Access to Microcredits and Financial Support for Small Producers, Promoting Sustainable Rural Entrepreneurship:

- Offering financial assistance to small-scale farmers through microloans and grants, helping them develop sustainable agricultural businesses.

Thanks to these efforts, many families have managed to increase agricultural production, generate surplus to sell in local markets, and strengthen the community economy. This has created a virtuous cycle of progress and self-sufficiency.

Basic Education and the Full Development of Childhood

In disadvantaged rural areas, access to basic education is one of the main challenges for human development. Christian organizations, in collaboration with local churches, have launched educational programs focused on ensuring that children and youth in these communities have real opportunities to progress. These initiatives aim to bridge the education gap by providing resources, infrastructure, and support to help young people achieve their potential and break the cycle of poverty. Through these efforts, Christian organizations are playing a key role in creating long-term opportunities for personal and community growth.

The projects include:

Construction and Equipping of Community Schools with Resources Adapted for Rural Environments:

- Building and equipping schools in rural areas with the necessary resources to create effective and sustainable learning environments.

Literacy Programs for Children and Adults, Significantly Reducing Illiteracy Rates:

- Providing literacy programs that target both children and adults, helping to decrease illiteracy in underserved areas.

Christian Values Education that Promotes Solidarity, Respect, and Social Responsibility:

- Incorporating instruction in Christian values, focusing on the development of key virtues such as solidarity, respect, and social responsibility.

Scholarships and Educational Support for Low-Income Families, Preventing School Dropout:

- Offering scholarships and financial support to ensure that children from low-income families can stay in school and continue their education.

Thanks to these initiatives, the outlook for hundreds of rural communities has completely transformed, giving new generations access to a more dignified future filled with opportunities.

Impact on Society and Community Consolidation

The success of these projects goes beyond personal improvements, as they have driven processes of social transformation and the strengthening of community ties. Local churches function as coordinating centers, fostering dialogue between families, organizations, and community leaders.

Collaboration has promoted values such as solidarity, shared responsibility, and participatory leadership, strengthening more cohesive and resilient communities in the face of economic, environmental, and social challenges.

Moreover, these initiatives have helped reduce forced migration from rural areas to cities or abroad by creating real opportunities for local economic development.

Community Reconstruction: Haiti After the 2010 Earthquake

On January 12, 2010, Haiti was struck by a devastating 7.0 magnitude earthquake that killed over 220,000 people, injured hundreds of thousands, and left approximately 1.5 million homeless. This disaster destroyed much of the country's infrastructure; hospitals, schools, homes, and government buildings collapsed under the quake's impact, plunging the country into an unprecedented humanitarian crisis.

Amid this landscape of suffering and despair, both local and international Christian churches emerged as key players in the immediate response and long-term process of community reconstruction. Christian faith went beyond offering prayer or spiritual comfort; it became an organized and sustainable force that saved lives and laid the foundation for the country's social and economic recovery.

Churches as Places of Support and Refuge

When the government system and basic services collapsed, Christian churches emerged as the main centers of community coordination. Thanks to their strong presence in neighborhoods, rural areas, and remote communities, these churches became key places for providing comprehensive assistance. They not only offered immediate relief but also organized efforts for long-term recovery, ensuring that those most affected by the disaster received the support they needed. By leveraging their networks and local relationships, churches played a central role in restoring a sense of order and hope in the midst of chaos.

The actions taken were:

Church Facilities Adapted as Temporary Shelters to Host Displaced Families:

- Church buildings were converted into temporary shelters, providing a safe haven for families who had been displaced by the earthquake.

Distribution of Food and Drinking Water, Managing National and International Donations:

- Churches coordinated the distribution of essential supplies, including food and clean water, managing both national and international donations to support affected communities.

Primary Healthcare Services Through Volunteer Brigades, Often Collaborating with International Christian Missions:

- Volunteer medical brigades offered primary healthcare services, frequently collaborating with international Christian missions to provide essential medical care to survivors.

Spaces for Emotional and Spiritual Support, Offering Pastoral Care to Those Who Had Lost Loved Ones or Their Livelihoods:

- Churches created spaces for emotional and spiritual support, offering pastoral care to individuals who had lost loved ones or their means of livelihood.

The Christian Network in Haiti, Supported by International Organizations Such as World Vision, Compassion International, and Samaritan's Purse, Played a Crucial Role in Reaching Communities That Could Not Be Reached by Government Aid:

- The Christian network in Haiti, in partnership with organizations like World Vision, Compassion International, and Samaritan's Purse, played a key role in reaching remote communities that were inaccessible to government aid.

Education in Times of Crisis: Temporary Schools and Community Training

One of the most immediate challenges after the earthquake was ensuring access to education, as more than 80% of the schools in Port-au-Prince and its surrounding areas were destroyed or rendered unusable. To address this situation,

Christian churches established temporary schools in tents, courtyards, and community facilities. These makeshift schools provided children with the opportunity to continue their education, even in the aftermath of the disaster, offering a sense of stability and hope for the future.

The result of these initiatives was:

Restore Educational Continuity for Thousands of Children and Adolescents:

- Temporary schools ensured that children and adolescents could continue their education despite the devastation, preventing a long-term educational setback.

Incorporate Psychosocial Support Programs to Address Trauma and Promote Emotional Resilience:

- These programs helped children and families cope with the emotional toll of the disaster, supporting their recovery and promoting long-term resilience.

Train Community Leaders and Volunteer Teachers to Ensure Basic Education in Emergency Situations:

- Christian organizations trained local leaders and volunteers to provide education in emergency settings, ensuring that learning could continue under difficult circumstances.

Incorporate Christian Values in Rebuilding the Collective Identity to Strengthen Hope and Solidarity:

- By integrating Christian teachings on love, hope, and compassion, these initiatives helped communities heal and rebuild their sense of identity, fostering unity and mutual support.

These makeshift schools not only provided a sense of normality for the affected families but also protected children from additional dangers, such as recruitment by criminal groups, human trafficking, or labor exploitation.

Christianity in Action: From Prayer to Organization

The impact of Christian churches in Haiti went beyond immediate charitable actions. The severity of the disaster made it necessary to evolve from short-term humanitarian aid to a more structured organization focused on community reconstruction.

The values of the Kingdom of God, such as justice, mercy, integrity, service, and hope, inspired the development of sustainable programs. Among these are:

Safe and Durable Housing:
Churches, in collaboration with Christian NGOs, built homes that could withstand earthquakes and hurricanes.

Economic Development Projects:
Training in trades, support for microenterprises, and access to microcredit for impacted families were essential to restoring livelihoods.

Strengthening Community Health:
Mobile clinics and vaccination programs were implemented in areas with no access to hospitals, improving healthcare services.

Local Leadership Development:
Training in community management was provided to empower communities and encourage their involvement in decision-making processes.

This model demonstrated that Christian faith, beyond being merely an emotional comfort, can transform into an organizing force capable of mobilizing resources, coordinating efforts, and fostering structural changes.

Impact on Society and Community Strength

More than a decade after the earthquake, the results of the work carried out by churches and Christian organizations in Haiti are still evident:

Reduced Social Vulnerability:
Communities now have access to housing, education, and clean drinking water, significantly improving their living conditions and reducing their vulnerability to future crises.

Strengthened Community Cohesion:
The creation of spaces where victims, local leaders, and organizations worked together towards common goals has helped build stronger, more united communities, fostering a sense of shared responsibility and cooperation.

Preparedness for Future Disasters:
The implementation of early warning systems and response strategies linked to Christian community networks has enhanced the country's disaster preparedness, ensuring a quicker, more coordinated response in future emergencies.

Faith as a Driver of Resilience:
Rather than being passive, faith served as a driving force for resilience, turning despair into concrete actions for reconstruction, helping communities rebuild and find hope in the aftermath of the disaster.

Christianity and Sustainable Development

The case of Haiti demonstrates that the practice of Christianity goes beyond individual prayer. It is a faith that is structured, mobilized, and turned into concrete actions, working closely with communities, local governments, and international organizations.

This shows a model where the church acts as an active agent of sustainable development, combining spiritual values with social, economic, and educational strategies. The testimony of the Haitian church after the earthquake confirms that Christianity is not only not a barrier to progress but can also be a catalyst for comprehensive transformation.

Conclusion

History shows us that when faith and action complement each other, sustainable, inclusive, and equitable development is achieved. It is no coincidence that many of the most trusted institutions, such as schools, hospitals, and humanitarian organizations, have emerged from a Christian worldview.

The cases presented here are not isolated exceptions; in fact, they serve as models that could inspire today's nations. If Christianity was able to achieve so much during times of persecution, scarcity, or crisis, how much more could it accomplish if taken seriously by nations as an ethical and social guide?

CHAPTER SIX

Christianity and Social Commitment: A Faith That Acts, A Nation That Prospers

ONE OF THE FOUNDATIONS of genuine Christianity is social responsibility. It is not enough to simply have faith in God or live a personal spirituality confined to churches; a true follower of Christ carries their belief beyond, actively participating in the streets, hospitals, underserved communities, educational systems, and even within government structures.

In verses 13 and 14 of chapter 5 of Matthew, Jesus said:

You are the salt of the earth... You are the light of the world.

These metaphors are not merely passive; they imply presence, impact, and transformation. Salt preserves, heals, and adds flavor. Light illuminates, guides, and reveals. In other words, Christians have both a public and spiritual responsibility.

What does social responsibility mean from a Christian perspective?

Christian social responsibility involves a deliberate commitment to practice faith in ways that benefit others, especially the most disadvantaged, promoting justice, well-being, and love for one's neighbor. It is not merely about occasional acts of philanthropy; it is about consistently living according to the biblical mandate of service.

"For I was hungry and you gave me something to eat; I was thirsty and you gave me something to drink; I was a stranger and you took me in..." (Matthew 25:35)

This passage captures the essence of Christianity in practice. Faith goes beyond being just a doctrine; it translates into action. For this reason, many of the major social change movements throughout history have emerged from a deep Christian conviction.

Implications in the Social and Economic Spheres

When individuals, families, churches, and governments act based on a Christian ethics of social responsibility, positive results are generated, such as:

- Reduction of systemic poverty.
- Greater participation in the community and civic life.
- Strengthening of social support networks.
- Reduction of violence due to social abandonment.
- Promotion of volunteering, ethical activism, and restorative justice.

Additionally, a model of citizenship is promoted in which both duties and love have the same importance as rights.

Current Examples of Christian Social Responsibility

Churches as Dynamic Community Centers:

In many rural areas of Latin America, the church stands out as the only gathering point for community, educational, and cultural activities. It often fills the absence of the state by providing essential services. The Christian presence has facilitated the establishment of libraries, mobile clinics, community cleaning teams, literacy promotion campaigns, and solidarity initiatives like soup kitchens and shelters for those suffering from violence.

Businesses with Ethical Responsibility Based on Christian Principles:

In countries like Chile, Mexico, and the Dominican Republic, some Christian entrepreneurs have established businesses with an objective beyond profit: they aim to transform lives. They achieve this by offering employment to ex-convicts, promoting fair trade, respecting the environment, and sharing profits with social causes.

Christian Youth Groups Dedicated to Service:

Initiatives such as Un Techo para mi País, La Ola, and Juventud con una Misión mobilize thousands of young believers to build homes, teach classes, clean beaches, accompany the sick, and spread hope.

The Role of the Church in Social Change

The Church, conceived not only as an institution but also as a community of believers, plays a strategic role in regenerating the social fabric. Its duty is:

- A prophetic voice that denounces injustice.

The Church speaks out against societal wrongs, advocating for those whose voices are often ignored, and calling for justice in all areas of life.

- Hands at work, assisting those in need.

Beyond words, the Church engages in direct service, providing practical support to the vulnerable, whether through food, shelter, or healthcare.

- A bridge of reconciliation, restoring broken relationships.

The Church acts as a mediator, fostering peace and healing between individuals, communities, and even nations divided by conflict.

- A motor of service that organizes sustainable solutions for structural problems.
- The Church doesn't just address immediate needs; it organizes long-term strategies to tackle the root causes of poverty, inequality, and injustice.

When the Church limits itself to preaching without action, it loses its authority. However, when it acts with love, humility, and justice, it becomes a beacon of change.

Jesus, the Ultimate Example of Social Responsibility

Jesus did not establish a political party, but He challenged oppressive systems. He did not create an NGO, but He fed the multitudes, healed the sick, welcomed the excluded, and dignified women. His life was a living testimony that faith must address the wounds of the world.

"The Spirit of the Lord is upon me... He has sent me to heal the brokenhearted, to proclaim liberty to the captives, and recovery of sight to the blind..." (Luke 4:18)

Conclusion

The driving force behind every revolution is ideology. Trying to discuss transformations in a country without a solid ideological foundation would be a grave mistake, as ideology provides convictions, common sense, and direction to a nation. It is what nourishes citizens with the determination to fight for change, sharing faith, feelings, and common ideals. In short, it is thanks to ideology that collective visions and missions can be built, guiding the group forward together.

A country is not transformed solely through the approval of laws or the construction of infrastructure; these are necessary tools, but by themselves, they are insufficient. Real change occurs when citizens take responsibility for their commitment to the common good. In this context, ideology acts as a framework that aligns individual actions with the larger national goals.

Genuine Christianity has the power to form this type of citizenship. More than a religious belief, it offers a way of life that drives values such as solidarity, justice, respect, and love for one's neighbor. When these principles are applied in daily life, they produce responsible citizens with solid convictions, committed to the common good.

Therefore, social and national change is not limited to material aspects; it also demands a transformation of consciousness. Ideological convictions motivate people to persevere, act with consistency, and maintain unity of purpose even in the face of difficulties.

In summary, a nation that desires true transformation must rely on an ideology that unifies, motivates, and mobilizes its population. When that ideology is nourished by genuinely lived Christian principles, it becomes a powerful force capable of forming responsible citizens and guiding the country toward justice and sustainable development. The more a nation's administration resembles the Kingdom of God, based on justice, mercy, service, and truth, the greater its prosperity will be. This is because it will be built on eternal values that strengthen the moral, social, political, and economic aspects of the nation.

CHAPTER SEVEN

Separation of Church and State: A Barrier or an Opportunity?

IN MANY MODERN SOCIETIES, the expression "separation of church and state" is interpreted as a declaration of hostility toward the presence of faith in the public sphere. This perception has led to the marginalization of traditional moral values and a distrust of religious matters within government. However, this separation does not have to be an impediment. From a Christian perspective, it can offer an opportunity to purify the testimony of faith, maintain its integrity, and ensure its social influence without the need for coercive impositions.

Jesus Himself established the distinction between the civil and the divine when He said:

"Give to Caesar what is Caesar's, and to God what is God's." (Mark 12:17)

This statement does not seek to divide the human being into two parts (spiritual and civic), but rather calls to live with responsibility both toward the laws of the country and the eternal principles.

What Does the Separation of Church and State Really Mean?

The separation of church and state should not be interpreted as the exclusion of faith from the public sphere. Instead, it should be seen as a guarantee to ensure religious freedom and prevent potential abuses of power by both entities. More positively, this separation:

- Prevents the State from establishing an official religion.
- Protects churches from political influence.
- Ensures the right to freedom of expression and the practice of religion.
- Allows diverse beliefs to coexist within an environment of respect and legality.

Christian faith does not require political power to exert influence. Its impact comes from its ability to transform hearts and communities, rather than relying on decrees.

Dangers of a Fusion Between Church and State

Throughout history, instances where the Church has dominated the State or the State has manipulated the Church have led to:

Religious Persecutions Against Minorities or Dissidents:

When the Church and State are intertwined, it often leads to the persecution of those who do not conform to the dominant religion or belief system, silencing opposition and dissent.

Ethical Corruption within the Religious Institution:

A close relationship with political power can lead to corruption within religious institutions, as the Church may begin to prioritize political agendas over its spiritual mission, compromising its integrity.

Imposition of Religious Practices Without Conviction:

When political power is linked with religious institutions, individuals may be forced to adhere to religious practices or beliefs without genuine conviction, undermining the essence of faith.

Social Rejection of Religion Due to Unpopular Political Associations:

If the Church is closely associated with political regimes or parties, especially those that are unpopular, it can lead to a societal rejection of the faith, as people may see it as a tool of political control rather than a spiritual guide.

Christianity loses credibility when it unconditionally aligns itself with political parties or governments, neglecting its prophetic vocation to correct and denounce any injustice, regardless of its origin.

Opportunities in a Secular State

A well-interpreted separation allows Christians to actively engage in political and social life without having to exert control over power. This opens up opportunities such as:

Forming citizens with a Christian ethical conscience that enables them to influence laws, institutions, and policies from their faith, but without imposing it.

Forming interreligious and secular coalitions to jointly address social issues such as poverty, violence, human trafficking, or corruption.

Contributing to the nation's progress from outside the power structure, acting as a guide and example in all areas: education, health, economy, justice, culture, and media.

Latin America: Between Tensions and Possibilities

In many countries in Latin America, the principle of a secular state has sometimes been used to limit the influence of Christian voices, particularly in discussions on values, family issues, or education. However, this same concept has also played a crucial role in preventing religious authoritarianism and protecting minorities.

In Colombia, Chile, and Mexico, Christian leaders have had a notable impact on public life without having to impose their faith through laws. In Haiti and the Dominican Republic, although there is a strong religious syncretism, Christian churches have retained their ability to influence socially and morally, independent of the State.

Jesus Christ never became involved in politics, but He was always present among the people.

Jesus did not seek positions of power, but His voice left a mark on the authorities. He questioned systems, exposed hypocrisies, valued the invisible, and modeled leadership based on service. He didn't need a seat in the Senate to transform history; from His principles, sown with conviction, He built the Kingdom of God without resorting to force.

"My kingdom is not of this world." (John 18:36)

This does not mean He lacked impact in this world. Rather, His essence lies not in dominating, but in transforming both internally and externally through love, truth, and justice.

Conclusion

The proper separation of church and state does not oppose Christianity; rather, it provides a conducive environment where faith can be genuine, free, and vigorous without turning into a political tool.

Instead of detaching from the country, Christians should be more involved than ever with their nation. Not to establish a theocracy, but to reflect the values of the Kingdom in all areas of society. When the Church remains faithful to its mission and the state respects religious freedom, both can work towards the common good from their unique but complementary roles.

CHAPTER EIGHT

The Role of the Church in Times of Crisis: Shelter, Response, and Reconstruction

CRISES REVEAL THE HEART of nations. In the most critical moments, when governments fail, economic systems collapse, or the social fabric unravels, the Christian Church has repeatedly proven to be a pillar of hope, organization, and service.

From the times of the early Church, which cared for the sick during the plagues of the Roman Empire, to present-day congregations offering shelter during earthquakes, wars, and pandemics, Christianity has shown that its faith does not shy away from suffering; rather, it confronts it with compassion and concrete actions.

Fundamental Roles of the Church in Times of Crisis

Spiritual and Emotional Sanctuary

In times of chaos, the Church provides comfort, moral guidance, and a sense of hope. Through prayer, community, preaching, and pastoral support, it helps individuals regain their dignity and find purpose in the midst of suffering.

The Lord is near to the brokenhearted and saves those who are crushed in spirit. (Psalm 34:18)

Urgent Humanitarian Response

Churches are often the first to respond when a disaster occurs. Being deeply integrated into their communities, they have the ability to quickly mobilize volunteers, distribute food, clothing, and water, and provide shelters without having to wait for bureaucratic processes.

Reconstruction of the Social Fabric

After the initial impact, the Church focuses on healing relationships, providing psychological support, rebuilding homes, and revitalizing local economies. This is especially relevant in areas where the presence of the State is weak or nonexistent.

Historical and Current Examples

The Church During World War II

In Europe, many Christian communities provided refuge to persecuted Jews, assisted prisoners, and offered support during the Nazi regime. Leaders like Dietrich Bonhoeffer in Germany and Corrie ten Boom in the Netherlands showed through their actions that genuine faith does not stay silent in the face of injustice. Their bravery not only saved thousands of lives but also demonstrated how the values of the Kingdom of God can persevere and transform even in oppressive and tyrannical contexts.

Haiti (2010) – Earthquake and Christian Mobilization

After the devastating earthquake that struck Haiti, when many government infrastructures collapsed, both local and international churches played a crucial role in the initial response. They provided shelter for thousands of people, distributed aid, and channeled international resources to those who needed them most. To this day, many reconstruction initiatives in the educational and housing sectors continue to be led by Christian organizations. This case illustrates how, during a crisis, values like compassion, service, and community can transcend state limitations to become key drivers of hope and community development.

Haiti in the Current Crisis: The Role of the Christian Diaspora

Currently, more than ten years after the earthquake that affected the country, Haiti faces one of its worst recent political, economic, and social crises. The growing insecurity, driven by control exercised by armed groups, has forced many local Christian churches to close their doors. As a result, many have lost essential spaces for spiritual and community refuge. However, in this challenging context, Christian churches in countries such as the United States, Canada, France, Brazil, Chile, Ecuador, and the Dominican Republic have become prophetic voices filled with solidarity from outside Haiti.

Far from their homeland, these communities do not remain indifferent: they are providing humanitarian aid, raising prayers, funding social initiatives, and, above all, acting as an alarm that awakens the consciousness of the Haitian people. Their message stresses that the nation must not resign itself to living under the weight of violence, corruption, and hopelessness. From abroad, the Christian diaspora seeks to revive faith, strengthen national identity, and remind the people that to truly rebuild Haiti, it is essential to begin with the hearts and consciences of its people.

Just as after the earthquake, the churches became a pillar of support, today, amid the political chaos and state paralysis, it is these voices in the diaspora that urge the return to the values of the Kingdom of God – justice, truth, solidarity, and hope – as the foundation for national rebirth. Their action demonstrates that even when insecurity silences temples within Haiti, Christian faith remains alive and active: mobilizing resources, forming consciences, and proclaiming that it is possible to transform Haiti.

Other Prophetic and Historical Examples of the Role of the Christian Diaspora

1. The People of Israel in Exile

In the Bible, the exile in Babylon represented one of the deepest crises in the history of God's people. Despite this, prophets such as Jeremiah and Ezekiel managed to keep hope alive from afar, urging their people to repentance and faithfulness toward God. It was during this period of diaspora that a nationalist spirit was revived, paving the way for their future restoration. Today, Haiti is experiencing a similar situation: it may be this active faith within its dispersed communities that serves as a prophetic echo, capable of stirring consciences and helping pave the way for a new, vibrant renaissance.

2. The African Diaspora and the Liberation Movement

During the centuries marked by slavery and colonialism, many Afro-descendant leaders in the diaspora played a crucial role in denouncing oppression and raising awareness of freedom. In Afro-Cuban and African American communities, the Christian faith not only offered spiritual hope but also became fundamental in driving social and political liberation movements. Thus, far from being an impediment, the diaspora acted as a powerful mobilizing force.

3. Martin Luther King Jr. and the Awakening of a Nation

In his own country, Martin Luther King Jr. symbolized what it means to be a prophetic voice capable of awakening collective consciousness. His message, based on biblical principles of justice and love, transcended the religious sphere to become a national and international call against racism and discrimination. Similarly, Haitian churches in the diaspora can transform into catalysts for a moral revival with impact beyond their borders.

4. South Korea and the Christian Influence in its Diaspora

After the Korean War and years of extreme poverty, the Korean diaspora played a crucial role by partnering with the Church to provide resources, education, and spiritual support to their nation. Today, South Korea is one of the most prosperous countries in Asia; this growth is attributed not only to economic efforts but also to the moral and community strengthening driven by the Christian faith.

Prophetic Conclusion

These examples demonstrate that when churches and Christian communities in the diaspora assume their role as watchmen, acting as sentinels who awaken the conscience of the people, they become a force capable of crossing borders and eras. In Haiti, a country burdened by political, social, and economic crises, it is precisely through its Christian diaspora that a voice akin to that of John the Baptist echoes from the desert: "Prepare the way of the Lord; make straight His paths."

The more the administration of Haiti, both internally and externally, aligns with the values of the Kingdom of God, the closer the country will come not only to achieving temporary relief but also to enduring and transformative prosperity.

COVID-19: The Church in the Global Pandemic

During the health crisis, Christian churches in countries such as Brazil, the Dominican Republic, Colombia, and the United States acted as vaccination centers. They also provided food and offered emotional and spiritual support to millions of people who were confined, isolated, or grieving. In the face of the limitations of government management of the situation, these religious communities offered closeness, solidarity, and companionship. This reminds us that true prosperity is not measured solely by the material resources available but also by the spiritual and emotional well-being of its inhabitants.

The Church as a Prophetic Guide and Defender

The Church also has the responsibility to denounce injustices that exacerbate crises, such as state negligence, corruption, abandonment of the poor, structural racism, and violence. If it only offers comfort without directly confronting evil, it loses its transformative capacity.

Jesus Himself, upon seeing the suffering of the crowds, wept with them, healed the sick, and gave them food. Then, He invited them to transform their lives. His example shows us that compassion and truth must go hand in hand.

Conclusion

Throughout history, it has been demonstrated that when the Church lives its faith with courage and commitment to service, it becomes a pillar of stability during times of collapse. It does not replace the State; rather, it complements it. Its goal is not to acquire power, but to create impact. In difficult times or crises, people need more than food, shelter, or medical care: they also need hope, guidance, and a sense of community.

A nation that recognizes and collaborates with a dynamic, autonomous Church committed to the common good becomes stronger. When faith is translated into action, what seems destroyed can be transformed into the foundation for rebuilding.

CHAPTER NINE

Conclusion: A Practical Approach for Countries Aspiring to Prosper

NATIONS DO NOT ARISE by chance, nor do they prosper solely due to their natural resources, technical skills, or political alliances. History shows that the greatness of a country is built upon the quality of its collective morality, the strengthening of its institutions, and the commitment of its people to fundamental principles. Christianity, when lived with integrity, provides precisely the set of essential values needed to achieve authentic, just, and sustainable development.

This book has examined how the Christian faith, instead of being an obstacle, can act as a force that sustains national well-being. From promoting a work ethic to driving an equitable economy, from fostering values in education to encouraging social responsibility, and from strengthening resilience in the face of crises to guiding political participation with wisdom, Christianity offers a holistic vision for both individuals and society as a whole.

"Righteousness exalts a nation, but sin is a reproach to any people." (Proverbs 14:34)

From a biblical perspective, justice transcends mere legality; it involves righteousness, compassion, fairness, and truth. Therefore, a nation built on the foundations of justice prospers, while straying from it leads to weakening.

Where to Head: Practical Guidelines for Governments, Churches, and Citizens

The transformation of a nation is not achieved through empty speeches or laws that ignore social reality, but through a clear vision focused on human dignity and justice. In this context, combining eternal principles with concrete actions is the path toward solid and sustainable development.

1. **For Government Authorities**

Legislate Without Fear of Acknowledging the Importance of Universal Christian Principles:

Truth, justice, respect for life, honesty, and service are values that strengthen social cohesion, not division. Embracing these principles in legislation helps create a society rooted in integrity, moral responsibility, and shared community values.

Invest in Ethical and Humanistic Education, Alongside Technical Knowledge:

Education that is void of moral principles leads to societies that are technically skilled but lack conscience. Investing in an education system that combines ethics, humanity, and technical training helps build individuals who are both competent and socially responsible.

Strengthen Collaboration with Christian Organizations:

Recognize and support Christian organizations that are effectively and transparently addressing the needs of the most vulnerable. The historical role of organized faith as a driver of social development should be acknowledged and further integrated into efforts to promote social justice and community well-being.

Safeguard Religious Freedom as the Foundation of a Strong Democracy:

A robust democracy depends on the freedom of its citizens to practice their faith. Protecting religious freedom ensures that the diversity of beliefs is respected while maintaining a unified commitment to values that transcend individual preferences.

Invest in the Agricultural Sector and Promote Food Sovereignty:

In countries like Haiti, with untapped resources in land and underground wealth, investing in modern and responsible agriculture is crucial. Developing the agricultural sector not only reduces dependency on foreign aid but also creates jobs, strengthens dignity, and promotes community stability. Ensuring food sovereignty helps local economies thrive and empowers communities to build sustainable futures.

2. **Regarding Churches**

Focus on Eternity Without Losing Sight of the Present: Promote Not Only Spiritual Salvation, but Also Social and Civic Responsibility.

Encourage Biblical Education for Pastors and Leaders:

It's essential that pastors and church leaders receive ongoing education that ensures their teachings align with the truth of the Scriptures, rather than personal interests. A faithful doctrine is crucial for the Church to continue being a guiding light and offering flavor to the world amidst social chaos.

Encourage Pastors to Have a Profession or Trade Outside the Church:

By encouraging pastors to have a vocation outside the Church, they won't be financially dependent on tithes and offerings. This approach helps prevent financial manipulation and reduces the risk of corruption. A pastor with a dignified and productive job can serve their community freely, offering a greater example of integrity.

Promote and Encourage Conscious and Responsible Motherhood:

Encouraging families to plan intelligently will reduce the number of abandoned children and strengthen the family as the fundamental pillar of society. By supporting responsible family planning, the Church can help create stronger, healthier communities.

Be Examples of Transparent Management and Community Service:

Demonstrating that the Christian faith is not a form of escape but a practical resource for building the common good.

Christians should show that their faith leads to responsible actions in both personal and public life.

Change the Perception That Christians Cannot Hold Political Roles:

The idea that a Christian cannot be a president, minister, or mayor should be challenged. In fact, politics benefits from leaders with strong principles. Leadership in politics requires more than charisma and technical skills; it requires judgment rooted in eternal values such as justice, truth, and service to others. Christian leadership in the political realm is not a personal benefit but a moral obligation to serve the entire nation.

For the Citizens:

Considering the family as the core of society means promoting marital stability, responsible parenting, and passing on spiritual and moral values to future generations. The family serves as the foundation for developing strong, ethical individuals and nurturing communities where justice, love, and responsibility thrive. By investing in the health and well-being of families, society as a whole can build a more resilient, compassionate, and prosperous future.

Promoting Sexual Education in Schools from an Ethical and Christian Perspective:

In the current scenario, characterized by rapid social changes, unlimited access to information, and transformations in family dynamics, comprehensive sexual education has become a necessity in schools. However, when this education is approached from an ethical and Christian perspective, it takes on a deeper and more holistic approach that goes beyond biological aspects by incorporating moral, spiritual, and social values essential for the complete development of the human being.

The primary goal of this approach is not only to provide information about sexuality but also to educate in principles and values. It seeks to help students understand human dignity, value their bodies, and recognize the importance of making responsible decisions related to their sexuality.

Principles of Christian Sexual Education:

Sexual education from a Christian perspective centers on the belief that the human body is a divine gift and views sexuality as a sacred aspect of being, intended to reflect love, dedication, and commitment. This approach is based on values such as:

Respect for Human Dignity:

Educating students to understand that their bodies and those of others are sacred and deserve to be treated with respect.

Self-Control and Personal Responsibility:

Teaching them to cultivate skills to make informed and mature decisions, avoiding impulsive or risky behaviors.

Love and Commitment:

Expressing sexuality as a manifestation of love that reaches its fullest expression within a stable, healthy, and committed relationship, such as in marriage.

Comprehensive Education:

Incorporating biological, psychological, emotional, spiritual, and social elements into the learning process to foster a balanced view of sexuality.

This approach is different from models of sexual education that are merely informational, as the latter focus solely on physical risks or the prevention of pregnancy and sexually transmitted diseases, neglecting the moral and emotional aspects.

Encouraging Respect for Our Own Bodies:

One of the key foundations of Christian sexual education is instilling in children and adolescents an appreciation for their own bodies as a fundamental part of their identity. This approach is based on biblical teachings, which affirm that humans were created "in the image and likeness of God" (Genesis 1:27), granting each person a unique and sacred nature.

Schools, in partnership with families, have the ability to promote:

Self-Esteem and Self-Knowledge:

Guiding students to understand and confidently accept the natural changes in their bodies during puberty.

Prevention of Sexual Abuse:

Teaching them to recognize healthy boundaries and identify inappropriate behavior to protect their physical and emotional integrity.

The Importance of Integrity and Personal Respect:

Fostering a lifestyle that values both the body and the decisions related to sexuality.

By strengthening students' connection to their own bodies, respect for others is also promoted, contributing to healthier, more empathetic, and responsible interpersonal relationships.

Promoting Responsibility in Individual Decisions:

The Christian perspective holds that sexuality involves freedom, but a responsible freedom linked to emotional and spiritual maturity. Therefore, it is important that sexual education in schools guides students to understand that each choice has personal, social, and spiritual implications.

This Method Focuses On:

Raising Awareness About Real Risks:

Clearly communicating the consequences of engaging in premature sexual relationships, including possible unwanted pregnancies, sexually transmitted infections, and emotional repercussions.

Development of a Life Plan:

Motivating students to think about their personal, academic, and spiritual goals, and understanding how their choices impact their future.

Reinforcing Personal Values:

Encouraging a sense of responsibility and self-control, promoting informed decisions that respect both their own dignity and that of others.

This type of education equips young people not only to avoid risks but also to make decisions that align with their values and personal goals.

Encouraging Waiting Until Marriage to Have Sex

From an ethical and Christian perspective, sexuality reaches its fullest expression within a stable bond, grounded in commitment and love: marriage. Sexual education provided in schools can collaborate with parents and religious communities to motivate students to delay engaging in sexual relationships until they reach emotional, psychological, and spiritual maturity that facilitates the building of more stable and healthy relationships.

This principle does not focus on imposition, but on providing educational guidance and values formation, promoting benefits such as:

- Greater emotional and affective stability in future relationships.
- Reduction of risks associated with unplanned pregnancies and sexually transmitted diseases.

- Promoting loyalty and commitment as the foundation of strong relationships.
  Fostering relationships based on respect and communication that transcend the physical.

  Thus, young people understand that sexuality is a complete expression of human love and not just a physical act driven by passing desires.

Cultural and Social Impact

Promoting sexual education with an ethical and Christian perspective in schools can have a positive impact on society as a whole, as it helps to:

- Reduce social issues such as teenage pregnancy, gender-based violence, and sexual exploitation.
- Develop responsible individuals with strong values and the ability to make informed decisions.
- Strengthen families by preparing new generations to form more stable and healthy relationships.
- Foster a culture of respect and dignity, where personal decisions are guided by both individual and community well-being.

This model incorporates the spiritual, moral, and social dimensions of the individual, offering a more comprehensive and sustainable approach to human development.

Sexual education from an ethical and Christian perspective does not aim to ignore the reality of sexuality but seeks to educate responsible, free individuals who are aware of their dignity. Teaching respect for one's own body, promoting responsibility in personal decisions, and encouraging waiting until marriage for sexual relations are principles designed to foster more stable, healthy, and lasting bonds.

Far from being a hindrance, this perspective provides schools with a solid foundation to guide students in the full development of their identity, supporting them to face current challenges with maturity and purposeful living.

Commit to productive work, especially in areas such as agriculture, fair trade, and small businesses, recognizing that development begins with personal responsibility.

Actively engage in democratic life by denouncing corruption, demanding transparency, and responsibly exercising the right to vote as an act of faith and civic commitment.

A Renewed Hope for the People

True development is not limited to building roads, erecting buildings, or establishing international agreements. Genuine progress occurs when a country fosters upright citizens, values the dignity of every human life, and understands that economic success is meaningless without justice.

Christianity has the power to transform culture, inspire changes in laws, humanize the economy, and heal deep social wounds. This is not achieved through imposition, but through the example, service, and integrity of those who practice it.

"If my people, who are called by my name, will humble themselves and pray, seek my face, and turn from their wicked ways; then I will hear from heaven, and will forgive their sin and heal their land." (2 Chronicles 7:14)

Conclusion

This book does not seek to merge Church and State or impose dogmas through decrees. Its goal is to make an urgent and hopeful call for nations to evaluate, without prejudice, the eternal principles of Christianity as the foundation for building more just, humane, and sustainable societies.

When the soul of a nation is based on truth, love, and compassion, its future ceases to be uncertain. It is then that faith becomes a driving force for development; hope turns into state policy; and justice becomes the most precious good of that nation.

Final Presentation to the Reader

I thank you for reaching this point. If this book has influenced your conscience, perspective, or beliefs, then its goal has already begun to be fulfilled.

I did not write these pages from a theoretical tower but from the ground where faith meets reality. Here, churches are not mere ornaments but sanctuaries for the soul; biblical principles go beyond rhetorical embellishments and act as guiding lights in our public lives. In this place, justice transcends a simple slogan: it is a sacred objective.

My greatest desire is that what you have read transcends paper. May these ideas materialize in your decisions, conversations, work, and community. I hope you are encouraged to be an agent of hope, an ambassador of the Kingdom, and a builder of the future.

Because the world does not need more experts, but more brave Christians.

And nations do not need more promises: they need more principles.

If we trust that it is possible and act with obedience, we will see our lands heal, prosper, and shine. On that day, we will all say: it was the Lord who did it, and in our eyes, it has become marvelous.

GLOSSARY

Christianity: A system of faith and way of life based on the teachings of Jesus Christ, with the Bible as its central axis, practiced by millions through various traditions over time.

Biblical Justice: A concept that encompasses not only legal aspects but also moral, ethical, and social dimensions. It involves equity, restoration, and the protection of the most vulnerable.

Stewardship: A Christian principle that teaches that everything we have, including money, resources, time, and talents, belongs to God and must be managed with wisdom and purpose.

Christian Ethics: A set of values and principles that guide a person's behavior according to the teachings of the Bible.

Church: A group of Christian believers. It can also refer to the organized institution or the universal spiritual body of God's people.

The Kingdom of God: A reality that is both spiritual and social, where divine values such as justice, peace, truth, love, humility, and service predominate.

Theocracy: A system of government in which religious leaders exercise political authority in the name of God. This book does not promote such a model.

Secular State: A political system that does not establish an official religion but ensures freedom of worship and allows religious individuals to participate in public affairs.

Christian Social Responsibility: The duty of believers to serve the community and contribute to the common good based on their faith, through concrete actions that promote justice and compassion.

Practical Living of the Gospel: Putting the message of Jesus Christ into action beyond words, manifested through acts of love, service, and justice within the social environment.

BIBLIOGRAPHY

Beisner, E. C. (s.f.). *Prosperity and poverty: The compassionate use of resources in a world of scarcity*. Crossway Books.

Campos, A. C. (2016). *La Reforma Protestante y su impacto social* [PDF]. Recuperado dehttps://www.ilco.cr/images/Libro/Reforma%20e%20impacto.pdf

Keller, T. (2010). *Justicia generosa: La gracia de Dios y la justicia social*. Andamio Editorial.

Mangalwadi, V. (2011). *El libro que dio forma al mundo: Cómo la Biblia creó el alma de la civilización occidental*. Editorial CLIE.

Padilla, C. R. (2001). *Misión integral: Ensayos sobre el Reino de Dios y la transformación de la sociedad*. Kairos Ediciones.

Richards, J. W. (2009). *Money, greed, and God: Why capitalism is the solution and not the problem*. HarperOne.

Stott, J. (2006). *La fe cristiana frente a los desafíos contemporáneos*. Editorial Caribe.

Volf, M. (2011). *Una fe pública: Cómo seguir a Jesús en un mundo pluralista*. Editorial Sal Terrae.

Weber, M. (2001). *The Protestant ethic and the spirit of capitalism*. Routledge.

Weber, M. (1968). *Economy and society*. Bedminster Press.

White, S. C. (1997). *Doing theology and development: Meeting the challenge of poverty*. Saint Andrew Press.

Barro, R. J., & McCleary, R. M. (2003). *Religion and economic growth* (NBER Working Paper No. 9682). National Bureau of Economic Research. https://www.nber.org/papers/w9682
Graham, A. (2022). *The underlying role of Christianity in political and social movements*. University of North Carolina. Recuperado de https://cdr.lib.unc.edu/concern/articles/dn39xb264?locale=en
Swart, I., & Nell, E. (2016). Religion and development: The rise of a bibliography. *HTS Teologiese Studies / Theological Studies, 72*(4), 1-12. https://doi.org/10.4102/hts.v72i4.3528
Noell, E., Smith, S., & Webb, B. (2013). *Economic growth*. En T. Stackhouse (Ed.), *The Oxford handbook of Christianity and economics* (pp. 103-120). Oxford University Press.
Oxford University Press. (2014). *The Oxford handbook of Christianity and economics*. Oxford University Press.
Thomas, A., & Reader, M. (Eds.). (s.f.). *The Elgar companion to development studies*. Edward Elgar Publishing.
Christian Perspectives on Property and Socio-Economic Development in Africa. (2003). Nairobi: CUEA Publications.
Pilgrim Press. (1994). *Sustaining the common good: A Christian perspective on the global economy*. Pilgrim Press.
Documentos de Fe y Alegría, Visión Mundial y World Vision. (s.f.). *Educación, desarrollo comunitario y servicio cristiano*. Recuperado de https://www.wvi.org
Associated Press. (2023, 22 de agosto). *From MLK to today, the March on Washington highlights the evolution of

activism by Black churches*. AP News. https://apnews.com/article/d4a207502d935a3272eea8a42a9f4a5a
King Institute at Stanford University. (s.f.). *Introduction | The Martin Luther King, Jr. Research and Education Institute*. Recuperado de https://kinginstitute.stanford.edu/introduction
Teachy.ai. (s.f.). *La Reforma Protestante y sus impactos*. Recuperado de https://teachy.ai/es/libros/educacion-secundaria/secundaria-1-grado/historia-a-espanol/la-reforma-protestante-y-sus-impactos-d32be
Time. (2018, 4 de abril). *10 historians on what people still don't know about Martin Luther King Jr.* TIME. https://time.com/5197679/10-historians-martin-luther-king-jr/
Wired. (2007, 15 de enero). *MLK: Have faith, be fair*. Wired. https://www.wired.com/2007/01/mlk-have-faith-be-fair/
La Biblia. (s.f.). *Santa Biblia*. Versión Reina-Valera, Nueva Versión Internacional (NVI) u otra traducción confiable.

ACKNOWLEDGMENTS

To God, my infinite source of wisdom and hope, to whom I dedicate every word in these pages.

To my wife, Dr. Andromarque Hilaire Jean-Pierre, companion in life and faith: thank you for your unconditional love and constant support.

To my parents, Mrs. Cereste Hilaire Raymond and Mr. Jean Virgilan Hilaire, for having given me an education grounded in the principles of Christianity.

To my children, Miss. Djessy-Naïra Hilaire Jean-Pierre and Mr. Romel Stevens Hilaire Jean-Pierre, for their faith in me and for accompanying me in this dream.

To my sisters and brothers, both by blood and in Jesus Christ, companions in faith and hope with whom I share the call to serve and transform.

To my fellow pastors, for their patience and their prayers, and to all those who, by their example or faith, have reminded me of the transformative power of the light of the Gospel over the world.

Made in the USA
Coppell, TX
04 January 2026

68086780R00066